Dear Anna,

So nice to hear
you perform today!
Keep up the great
work!

ONE STONE TO THE BUILDING
HENRIETTE RENIÉ'S LIFE THROUGH HER WORKS FOR HARP

JAYMEE HAEFNER

authorHOUSE®

AuthorHouse™
1663 Liberty Drive
Bloomington, IN 47403
www.authorhouse.com
Phone: 1 (800) 839-8640

Published by AuthorHouse 06/07/2017

ISBN: 978-1-5246-8513-3 (sc)
ISBN: 978-1-5246-8511-9 (hc)
ISBN: 978-1-5246-8512-6 (e)

Library of Congress Control Number: 2017904740

Dedicated to Mom and Dad:
for leaving the harp by the Christmas tree all those years ago,
and for believing in me even when I didn't believe in myself...
Thank you!

TABLE OF CONTENTS

FOREWORD

It was a privilege for me to serve as Jaymee Haefner's major field professor during her doctoral studies at Indiana University Jacobs School of Music. It was a special joy for me to share with her memories of my studies with Mademoiselle Renié. She then chose to write her thesis on Renié, after first translating a small book written in French about Renié by her dear friend and former student la Contesse Odette de Brye de Montesquiou. A previous biography, which was written by her goddaughter, Françoise des Varennes, was translated with help from me and French speaking students. However, both of these books, while giving wonderful informative details about Renié, still did not serve as definitive, scholarly biographies. So, this book by Dr. Haefner will secure for future generations a much-needed resource. My heartfelt congratulations to her for this remarkable work!

Susann McDonald
Bloomington, Indiana
January 7, 2017

PREFACE

At a young age, I noticed that Renié's name was uttered with special reverence by my harp teachers. From my first harp lesson with Anna Vorhes to studies with Kathy Bundock-Moore and Carrol McLaughlin, I learned about the compositions and the harp method taught by Renié, this petite giant in the harp world. When studying for my doctorate, the genius of Renié came into full view as a gentle but steady force which guided each set of hands that trained in Susann McDonald's studio at Indiana University Jacobs School of Music in Bloomington. Perhaps this trajectory was even more apparent because my teachers were sequential pupils of each other (Vorhes studied with McLaughlin, who studied with McDonald, who studied with Renié). I suspect that the marks of Renié's teaching would have been present, regardless of this direct connection.

Driven by a thirst to better understand the high regard that Susann McDonald had for Henriette Renié's work, I completed my dissertation research in 2006. At the time, I could have never predicted that this research would so utterly connect me to the world of harpists who came before me. I became accustomed to hearing the stories of Renié and was curious about the contrasting sides of her personality. She was a devout Catholic who wrote daily meditations and was simultaneously fascinated by the dark tales written by Edgar Allan Poe. While she spent much of her life teaching and practicing indoors, she also had a clear reverence for nature as depicted in her *Deux promenades matinales.* This woman who loved and cared so deeply for her god daughter made a conscious decision to never marry and to instead devote her life to "her harp."[*]

As we celebrate Susann McDonald's eightieth birthday and her enormous contributions to the harp world, I've witnessed a simultaneous resurgence of enthusiasm about Renié. Affectionately, Renié called Susann McDonald "ma petite Sue." Susann McDonald has tirelessly continued Renié's legacy. In this way, this book celebrates both beloved teachers who elevated so many students to a professional level. This connection exists between the many students of Mademoiselle Renié who established the harp's stature long before the current generation of harpists and Susann McDonald's students who are active in today's international harp community.

As Renié wrote in her method, we each come along to add our "stone" to building the foundation of the harp, and with it we pay homage to the transformational harpists who have paved the way

---

[*] Throughout Renié's papers, she referred to "her harp" in quotes when she wrote about her work. This had a special reverence, as the harp was not only an instrument to Renié, but a beloved friend.

for our work. This publication is a work of gratitude for each of those stones which work in harmony to support the building of the harp's history. While this work is not intended to be an exhaustive review of all Renié's works, it represents some of her most beloved works which illustrate her tripartite career as virtuoso, composer and teacher.

Jaymee Haefner
Denton, Texas
December 27, 2016

ACKNOWLEDGEMENTS

I would like to thank many people for their support throughout both phases of this publication. I am indebted to my teacher Susann McDonald for her incomparable guidance of my studies and research, as well as Elzbieta Szmyt, Professor of Harp. I would like to thank Professor Helga Winold and Professor Michael Schwartzkopf. Without their advice, this project would not have been possible. I would like to thank David Day and the entire staff at the International Harp Archives at Brigham Young University in Provo, Utah for their assistance in locating so many of the valuable documents belonging to Henriette Renié. As harpists, we are very fortunate to have so much history preserved in one location. I am thankful to Claire Renaud for her translation of the materials from the Renié archives, and to Elizabeth Huntley, editor of the *American Harp Journal* for the use of photographs.[*] Thanks also to my sister, Robyn Schmuck for proofreading and my brother, Tobin Schmuck, for allowing me to share his beautiful painting on the front cover, combined with graphic design by Brad Haefner. I would like to express my gratitude to Professor David Lasocki for his suggestions in the compilation of Henriette Renié's works and transcriptions. Above all, I am grateful to my husband, son and family for their unwavering support throughout my studies, research and career.

---

[*] All photographs are public domain unless otherwise listed.

CHAPTER 1:
RENIÉ'S BACKGROUND

> I am far from changing all the opinions of the past, although modern music has need of a special technique which is more extensive and more "supple" in order to adapt it. I do not pretend to give the final decisive word in the instruction of the harp. Others will probably come after me to add their one stone to the building. I only hope that my long experience will be an aid to them and a new point of departure.
>
> —Henriette Renié

Virtuoso, Composer, Teacher. Henriette Renié achieved the epitome of artistry in each of these arenas, not only in the eyes of her students and family, but to the acclaim of the musical French culture during the late nineteenth and early twentieth centuries. This humble and devout woman truly established a fundamental connection between many elements during her lifetime and today's harpists owe much to her.

As a virtuoso Mademoiselle (Mlle) Renié[*] established the harp for the first time as a respected solo instrument, which led in part to the development of acknowledgment for female artists during the late nineteenth and early twentieth centuries. She won the Prix

---

Opposite: Henriette Renié as an infant with mother, Gabrielle Marie Mouchet.

Epigraph. From Renié's *Complete Method for Harp.*

[*] Throughout this book, the abbreviation "Mlle" will be used for "Mademoiselle." During Renié's lifetime, it was customary for her students to address her with this title.

du Disque for her Odéon recording of *Danse des lutins*, with all the copies selling out within six months of its release.[1] As a composer, she left a myriad of masterpieces in her wake, including such virtuosic compositions as *Ballade fantastique* and *Légende*. She influenced several composers of her time, including Maurice Ravel, Claude Debussy and Camille Saint-Saëns. In turn, she influenced some of the most important compositions that came into the harp's repertoire during and after her lifetime. As a teacher, she not only developed the most thorough method for the double-action pedal harp, but contributed to the fundamental core of harp repertoire through her twelve volumes of transcriptions and original pedagogical works, which include *Feuillets d'album* and *Six pièces brèves* (op. 2).

Perhaps Mlle Renié's most striking contribution to the harp is her unparalleled devotion to furthering the study of other harpists. She passed on her profound wisdom and affection to her extremely successful students, who became some of the most influential performers and teachers. In this way, her passion continues to inspire current harpists.

With so many talents to offer and share, she remained remarkably modest, attributing all her gifts to her Creator. Never did she step before the public without breathing a prayer that her performance should glorify God.[2] As conveyed in her meditation from 10 December 1927, she believed that her mission was "to pass lightly through this world, scarcely putting a foot down." [3] Nonetheless, her imprint on the musical world has been deeply felt. The contributions to harp repertoire that she left were truly groundbreaking. Her love for the beauty of music and the harp were braided together, strengthening her influence and devotion to this instrument. By examining Renié's life works through her three-part mission as virtuoso, composer and teacher, we can gain a more complete understanding of this legendary harpist.

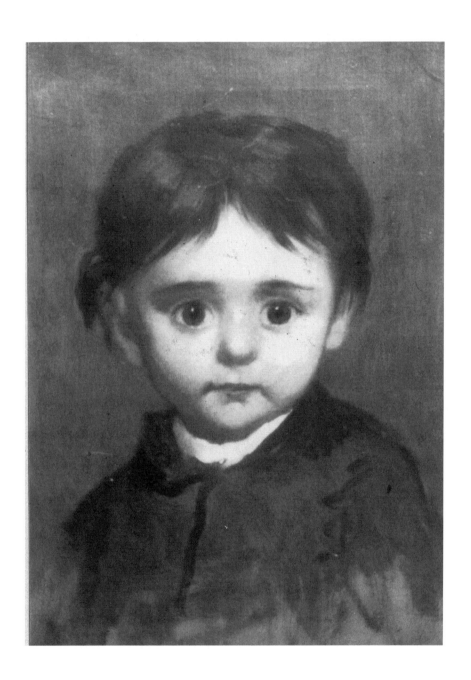

Brief Biography

Henriette Gabrielle Marie Sophie Renié was born on 18 September 1875 to Jean-Émile Renié and Gabrielle Marie Mouchet.[4] She was the youngest of five children, the first daughter born to the couple. Artistry was in Henriette Renié's genes. Her mother, Gabrielle Marie Mouchet, was a descendant of the well-respected Parisian cabinet-maker Joseph Desmalter. Henriette's father, Jean-Émile Renié, possessed many artistic talents as an architect, painter and singer. He followed his father's trade as an architect and was even a candidate for the Prix de Rome.* He longed, however, to be a painter and left his former profession after his father's death.[5] To maintain a steadier income than that of a painter, Jean-Émile frequently toured as an actor-singer. Gioachino Rossini admired Jean-Émile's bass voice so much that he later hired him for the Opéra of Paris.[6] Thereafter, Jean-Émile continued to perform and tour. When he proposed to marry Gabrielle Marie Mouchet, her father insisted that Jean-Émile leave his acting career to pursue a career as a painter. He studied under Théodore Rousseau; Jean-Émile's talent was such that many of his paintings were mistaken for those of his masterful teacher. During this time,

---

Opposite: Henriette Renié, 18 months old. Painting by her father, Jean-Émile

* A highly prestigious prize, the Prix de Rome was established in 1803 by the French government to reward painters, sculptors, architects, and musicians with a period of study in Rome.

he continued to sing in various venues and *soirées* to provide enough income for his family.[7]

At one such performance in Nice, Henriette was the delicate age of five when she heard her father sing in a concert at which the Belgian harpist Alphonse Hasselmans played. Hasselmans, at six feet and two inches tall, was a towering giant both physically and as a figure in the harp world. There is no doubt that he was shocked when on the train ride home from the concert, Jean-Émile's petite five-year-old daughter announced to them: "That man is going to be my harp teacher." With a combination of surprise and amusement, Hasselmans simply replied, "When you are bigger, we shall see, Mademoiselle!"[8]

After that serendipitous evening, the young Renié studied piano for three years, after which she began her harp lessons with Hasselmans. At the age of eight, her legs were not yet long enough to operate the harp's pedals, so her first year of playing was spent primarily on exercises which did not require pedal changes.[9] Renié's goddaughter, Françoise des Varennes, later recounted how Henriette became accustomed to "the gymnastic feat of hopping off of her chair to move a pedal on the right or one on the left without any break in the music, much to the amusement of her fellow school-mates, whose laughter Henriette considered foolish."[10]

Renié's progress on the harp was incomparable and she continued to take harp lessons with Hasselmans at the Érard* harp workshop on Rue du Mail because this location was nearer the Renié residence than the Conservatoire national supérieur de musique de Paris.[11] Her father soon developed pedal extensions for her, created from metal shafts of varying lengths attached to each pedal.[12] This allowed her to play a more varied repertoire on the harp after spending her first year restricted to diatonic exercises with no chromaticism or pedal changes.[13] From the beginning, Hasselmans held the highest expectations for the young girl. After a particularly difficult master class, he explained his reasoning to her: "You must be an example for the class, because I expect more from you than the others. That is why I seem so hard to please. . . ."[14]

With this encouragement, she became a student at the Conservatoire at the age of ten (during Hasselmans's first year as Professor of Harp), and she audited such subjects as counterpoint and sight-singing in addition to her harp practice.[15] She entered the 1885 *concours* (competition), hoping at least for an honorable mention. The jury was unanimously pleased with her performance and wished to offer her the formidable *premier prix* (first prize), but Ambroise Thomas, the director of the Conservatoire, felt that

---

* Érard was a French instrument manufacturer, focusing primarily on piano and harp manufacturing. Érard's first harp mechanism patent was filed in 1794.

she was too young for such a title. Winning the *premier prix* would have deemed the youthful Renié as a professional in her field and ineligible for further harp lessons at the Conservatoire. She was consequently awarded the *second prix* (second prize) at the same time as harpist Samuel Merloo.[*][16] She needed to wait only a short while for her well-deserved *premier prix,* which she received at the *concours* in July of 1887,[†] unanimously winning this title for her performance of the *Concertino for Harp and Orchestra* by Oberthür.[17] This was later described as one of the three greatest events in the history of the Conservatoire.[18] The details of this performance, recounted by Françoise des Varennes in a series of French radio programs, show Mlle Renié's charming innocence and humility at the tender age of twelve.

> Once on stage, Henriette experienced that phenomenon which marks a true virtuoso: a strangely increased sense of self-possession. She brought out her stool, which was nearly as high as she was tall, and made herself comfortable. As the string quartet began its opening measures, she suddenly noticed that her sky-blue knee-high stocking had fallen down around her ankle! She was fascinated by it. Normally

---

[*] Samuel Merloo again received the *second prix* in the competition of 1887, and was soon appointed as Professor of Harp at the Brussels Conservatory.

[†] Some confusion exists concerning Mlle Renié's age during the competition, and the competition date. Govea cites 1886 as the date for the competition, though many newspaper articles and Renié's biographies indicate that it occurred in 1887 before she turned twelve.

her clothing was very plain, sometimes it was even borrowed from her brothers. At the first tutti, she put the harp down and swiftly pulled up her stocking, much to the delight of the public and the press.

. . . Pandemonium broke loose. . . Henriette gathered that she had won the *premier prix*, but slightly bewildered by such an unusual explosion of enthusiasm, she backed off the stage, accompanied by the laughter of the crowd. The audience called for her reappearance as if they were cheering a great artist.

. . . Abashed at having behaved inappropriately, and feeling ridiculous, Henriette blushed and stood stock still. The crowd finally calmed down enough to hear Thomas announce emphatically: "Mademoiselle, the jury has unanimously awarded you the *premier prix*."

One of [the critics] concluded thus: "Ah! Petite Renié! In the future, don't pull your stockings up in public, Mademoiselle."[19]

Shortly after receiving this highest honor, Renié was presented with many opportunities. One of these was an invitation to perform for Queen Henriette of Belgium, who was so moved by her music that she presented Renié with a jeweled pin, decorated in red, white and blue (France's colors). Later, she had the honor of performing for Princess Mathilde* and the Emperor of Brazil.[20]

Almost immediately after receiving her *premier prix*, the twelve-year-old Renié was approached by students wishing to absorb some of her profound knowledge. Already by this time

---

* Princess Mathilde was the cousin of Napoleon III.

she had teaching experience, for when she was just nine years old Renié began teaching a friend of one of her older brothers, Ferdinand Maignien.* At that young age, she sometimes mimicked Hasselmans's sternness by slamming an etude book shut when she was not pleased with Maignien's progress, after which she would run outside and call back to him, asking if he wanted to play.[21]

As she grew, her musical skills were further honed when she was admitted to the Conservatoire de Paris to study harmony at age thirteen. This was a year before the normal age of admittance, but an exception was made for her.[22] Classes in fugue and composition followed, in which Mlle Renié was the first young girl to be included.[23] Soon, she won Conservatoire prizes for her compositional skills. In 1891, she was awarded the Prix de Harmonie, and in 1896 she received the Prix de Contrepoint Fugue et Composition.[24] She studied fugue and composition with Charles Lenepveu and Théodore Dubois and during one of these classes in 1895, she revealed her first composition for harp and violin: *Andante religioso*. Despite the encouragement she received from Ambroise Thomas and Jules Massenet, she was especially nervous about showing her composition to her eighteen classmates, all of whom were men. She carried her composition in her briefcase for six weeks and finally decided to share it on a day when many

---

* Many years later, Ferdinand became the harpist for the Paris Opéra.

of her classmates were absent. When she did, Théodore Dubois enthusiastically declared, "It's very good. You should do many more like that!"[25]

This moment marked the dawning of the second phase in Mlle Renié's career—as a composer. Shortly after, she began writing her *Concerto en ut mineur.* Théodore Dubois was so excited about her work that after she completed it in 1901, he encouraged her to share it with Camille Chevillard, the director of the famed Lamoureux Orchestra (or Concerts Lamoureux).[26] Renié's triumphant premier of her Concerto with the Lamoureux Orchestra was a landmark success for both the harp as a solo instrument and female musicians; she was one of the first women to receive applause simultaneously as soloist and composer.[27] This performance opened numerous paths to her success as a virtuosic soloist in France and surrounding countries. Soon, Renié was invited to play her famed Concerto twenty-five more times in Europe.[28] She lived in an era when few women were recognized in the musical arena, but her musicianship immediately put her beyond any preconceptions of gender or instrument limitation. In fact, her success spurred new harp compositions by many respected composers: Théodore Dubois, Gabriel Pierné, Claude Debussy and Maurice Ravel, for example.[29]

In Paris, Renié was surrounded by some of the most famous musicians and composers of the era, and her influence upon them

was notable. In 1912, Hasselmans came to her and asked if she
would take over his class at the Conservatoire because he wished
to retire. Gabriel Fauré was the director, and Hasselmans conveyed
to Renié that he had spoken with Fauré about the wish for Mlle
Renié to become his successor. Fauré announced that despite
Renié's highest credentials, Marcel Tournier had been chosen
as Hasselmans's successor at the Conservatoire. Hasselmans
passed away that very evening, shortly after receiving this news at
dinner.[30]

Disciples of Henriette Renié may find it difficult to understand
how a harpist of her caliber would be denied the professorship.
Even though she was clearly a very strong candidate for the
position, the Conservatoire was not allowed to select her. During
that time, the French Third Republic was struggling to separate
religion and state; Renié was keenly involved in supporting
the Catholic Church. With other supporters, she would visibly
wear her cross and was registered as "Catholic and reactionary"
on the dossier of the state because of her courageous views.[31]
To be appointed as a professor at the Conservatoire de Paris
(a government institution), one had to be recommended by the
Ministry of National Education. Because of her dossier, Renié was
not approved.[32]

Despite this disappointment, she remained steadfastly devoted to her work and her deeply spiritual Catholic beliefs, which were her stronghold. She arose early each morning to spend time with her Lord, attending church at Soeurs du Saint-Sacrement (Sisters of the Blessed Sacrament) on Cortambert Street when she lived at her parents' home, and later at Notre-Dame de Passy.[33] After chapel she would record her meditations* in small notebooks, after which she would turn wholeheartedly to her work at the harp, preparing for upcoming concerts by working for two or three hours in a stretch and taking only short breaks.[34] She wished not to be interrupted for any reason and warned, "You may disturb me if the house catches on fire—not otherwise!"[35] The afternoons were spent teaching until about five o'clock, after which the evenings were filled with music composition and transcription.[36]

Mlle Renié always found time to write despite her extremely full schedule. Her notebooks of meditations and frequent letters to her students reveal her warm love of life. She conveyed her belief that with her performances, she was only returning her gifts to the One who bestowed them. In a letter written to one of her pupils, Odette de Montesquiou, Mlle Renié explained the purpose of performance:

---

* Mlle Renié's notebooks of meditations have been carefully preserved at the International Harp Archives at Brigham Young University in Provo, Utah.

The better I felt, the more I felt myself to be in full 'bloom,' the more I would suffer and choke up while thinking about the audition of April 2. . . . Naturally I wanted to have intelligence, memory, musical comprehension, technique, an uplifted soul and beauty of expression; I would have instinctively wished that all my work and all of my achievements were mine, with the divine gifts to do what I desired with them on April 2. Yet the presence of God is behind all of them: the gifts are talents that were made to bear fruit; both of them belong to God, I have known this for a long time . . . and yet it should be believed that I had forgotten these. And (finally) I have given everything, this entire burden of intellectual, spiritual, and other wealth. . . . In truth, I did not even so much give them as return them to Him who alone possesses.[37]

Renié's spirit of devotion, as conveyed by this letter, was witnessed not only by her students, but by other artists in the French musical community. Her benevolence was shown through her creation of the *Petite caisse des artistes* (Little Fund for the Artists) during World War I (1914–1918). Mlle Renié recognized that many of her comrades were in financial need. She created this fund to help them anonymously. Each month during World War I, a minimum of forty checks and encouraging notes were sent out to those in need.[38] Dressed in a long black velvet gown, she frequently played at benefit concerts to raise these funds.[39] She also founded *L'association des anciens élèves du Conservatoire* (The

Association for Former Pupils of the Conservatory) with Alfred Cortot.[40]

Mlle Renié found other charitable ways to inspire international harpists to begin successful careers. For example, she established the first international harp competition, the Prix Renié (or Concours Renié), which took place for the first time in 1914. She offered a large sum of money for the First Prize, and the jury included several internationally recognized composers, including Maurice Ravel, Gabriel Pierné and Charles-Marie Widor. After a lapse during World War I, the competition continued to take place in 1921, 1923 and 1926. Unfortunately, due to the vast costs of running such a competition, Renié was not able to continue. The idea, though, was passed on to Israel in 1959, and the competition continues to this day.[41] One of her most renowned students, Susann McDonald, furthered Renié's vision of an international harp competition. She founded the USA International Harp Competition in 1989, which is held every three years. This competition draws talented harpists from around the world to Indiana University in Bloomington.

Just before World War II, Renié traded her life of concertizing for the energy necessary to create her *Méthode complète de harpe,* commissioned by Alphonse Leduc.[42] To this day, these two volumes offer the most comprehensive description of Renié's harp technique, grounded in her belief in "suppleness." Leduc published this method in French and English, and is currently considering the publication of a Japanese edition. Through such translations of her method, Renié's teachings will continue to inspire harp students everywhere.

Henriette Renié spent sixty-nine years of her life tirelessly devoted to the harp's evolution. Her gifts were recognized by all who came to know her. For her high musical achievement she was presented with the "Salon of French Musicians" gold medal of 1935 in the great Conservatoire where her journey began.[43] For her tireless dedication to others in need, she received another great honor in 1954: she became one of the very few women appointed as a Knight in the *Légion d'Honneur.** Significantly, the preprinted salutation *Monsieur* on this letter was written over with the salutation "*Mademoiselle.*"[44] Renié was clearly deserving of this award, it was denied her for a long time because of the government dossier which labeled her as "Catholic and reactionary."[45]

One of her last performances took place in 1955 when several of her students gathered for her eightieth birthday to festively commemorate her achievements of setting new parameters for the harp and for female musicians.[46] Those who had the honor of

---

* The *Légion d'Honneur* was established in 1802 by Napoléon Bonaparte as a great honor for military or civil achievement.

knowing this extraordinary woman were deeply touched by her spirit of life, and those of us who did not have the privilege of meeting her personally are still affected by the imprint she left on the harp's current identity. Without her dedication, the harp would not have the status that it enjoys today. Upon her passing on 1 March 1956, Maurice Imbert[*] wrote:

> ... Truly with Henriette Renié has disappeared a great and noble figure of an artist of the present generation. The success which she achieved as virtuoso and composer in France as well as other countries makes for her the most beautiful of crowns.

After her passing, Renié's beloved goddaughter Françoise des Varennes preserved and furthered her legacy by speaking about Renié's lifework and music throughout the world.[47]

---

[*] Maurice Imbert was one of the most recognized Parisian music critics during Mlle Renié's lifetime.

Influence on the History of the Harp

In her lifetime, Renié was perched among several historical changes. The political climate in France was changing with the separation of church and state. Concurrently, the harp was just beginning to be recognized as a solo instrument. The world was in a state of turmoil and she witnessed both World War I and World War II. Surrounded by these circumstances, her appearance as a female virtuoso was a revolutionary achievement. On another level, Renié was tied into the construction of a new style of harp: the chromatic harp.

When the petite Renié first began her harp lessons with Alphonse Hasselmans, the double-action pedal harp was a comparatively young instrument patented in 1810 and produced by Érard. The double-action harp replaced the single-action harp, due to its added chromatic capabilities. Later single-action harps and double-action pedal harps had seven pedals, each controlling one note of the diatonic scale (C, D, E, F, G, A and B). These pedals are connected through the base of the harp to seven rods which run through the harp column, operating a mechanism located at the top of each string. The single-action harps had one row of hooks or discs which could shorten each string by a semi-tone. The pedals, in turn, had only two positions for flat and natural, or natural and sharp, depending on the tuning of each string.

Opposite: Henriette Renié, ca 1914, in the black velvet gown she wore while performing for benefits. (Image used with permission from the *American Harp Journal*)

The new Érard double-action harps, by comparison, had two rows of discs at the top of each string. With this mechanism, each string could be raised by one or two semi-tones, according to the position of the pedals (Diagram 1.1).

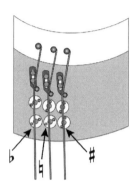

Diagram 1.1: Three harp strings with two rows of discs, illustrating the positions of flat, natural and sharp.[*]

This provided the new ability to play each string in flat, natural, or sharp by positioning the seven double-action pedals in one of three notches, allowing harpists to play in all keys (Diagram 1.2).

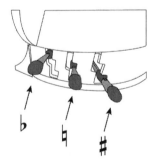

Diagram 1.2: Three pedals (D, C, and B) in the positions of flat, natural and sharp.

---

[*] Illustrations on this page used with permission by Bradley Haefner.

This new pedal mechanism provided harpists with the means to create enharmonic doublings on adjacent strings. For example, the harpist could set the C pedal into the sharp position (to sharpen all the C strings) and the D pedal into flat (to flatten all the D strings). In this way, the harpist could play the notes C♯ and D♭ (which sound identical in pitch) on adjacent strings. This opened a myriad of virtuosic capabilities for the harpist, including tremolo and glissando effects and a more varied repertoire.

The need for new capabilities arose from the increasingly chromatic repertoire of the Romantic era. While other orchestra and keyboard instruments were used to explore extended harmonies, the single-action pedal harp quickly became inadequate and was consequently ignored by many composers. Although the new double-action mechanism gave harpists more chromatic freedom, the pedals remained the most difficult aspect of performance.

Then in 1897, Renié inadvertently spawned the creation of a new rival to the Érard double-action harp. Before one of her performances she commented to Gustave Lyon, "Devil of an instrument! Oh! I wish it didn't have these pedals!"[48] Gustave Lyon, who worked for the French piano manufacturer Pleyel, Wolff and Company, replied to her by saying that he would make her a harp without pedals. This new instrument came to be called the "chromatic harp," or the "cross-strung harp" and was comprised of a total of seventy-six strings in two crossing rows.[49] Unfortunately, it lacked the resonance of the double-action harp and Renié preferred not to play it.

The following summer, Renié again found herself caught in the discourse between these two harp makers. The Érard harp and the new Pleyel chromatic harp were now in competition. Both companies had booths at the Brussels World Fair in 1897 and Renié was to showcase the Érard harp.[50] Due to an organizational error at the exposition, she found that her booth was set directly across from the Pleyel chromatic harp played by Édouard Risler. Knowing that Mlle Renié's tone on the double-action harp was superior in sound, he was careful never to play his chromatic harp at the same time she played. One day however, Renié staged a trick with one of her students, who asked Risler to play when he thought Renié had left her booth to take a break. As soon as he played his first chords, she suddenly returned and her marvelous tone wafted from her booth, drawing the crowd near her. Risler's sound on the chromatic harp obviously paled in comparison.[51]

These two harps rivaled each other in new compositions, especially between 1901 and 1906. M.A. Blondel, the director of Maison Érard, commissioned Maurice Ravel's *Introduction et allegro* for the double-action harp. This followed Pleyel's commission of Claude Debussy's *Danse sacrée et danse profane* for the chromatic harp.[52] Mlle Renié recognized the importance of this contribution to harp repertoire, and in 1910 she transcribed it for the double-action harp. Her transcription remains one of the most-performed works in the present-day repertoire for double-action harp. Other works originally written for chromatic harp, André Caplet's *Conte fantastique* for harp and string quartet, for instance, were soon transcribed for the double-action harp. Thus, the chromatic harp was stripped of several great works, giving the double-action harp the advantage by combining this masterful repertoire with the best timbre. Combined with Renié's addition of virtuosic compositions to the repertoire of the double-action harp, the Érard harp was elevated to an entirely new status.

CHAPTER 2:
RENIÉ AS VIRTUOSO

. . . My life is *exterior* by definition, by necessity, by obligation, and it has been for a long time!–To be a great virtuoso and a great artist, one must feel *deeply* but externalize what one feels; one must *give* without stopping; make contact with others; make their hearts and souls resonate by their encounter with one's own heart and soul, all given by one's art. . . .

—Henriette Renié

Henriette Renié's gifts for teaching and composing were intimately tied to her career as a prodigy at a young age. By winning the *premier prix* of the Conservatoire de Paris, she was deemed a professional. Her formal harp lessons at the Conservatoire ceased at that time, but Renié ardently continued to perfect her technique and presentation. Rather than attributing her success to her own diligent work, she would say that she was simply returning her talents to God.[53]

Her successes were many, and after one of her concerts her playing was brilliantly described in *L'art musical:* ". . . the Érard harp was simultaneously caressed and attacked, softly and then

---

Opposite: Henriette Renié's hand, 1954, photo by Mildred Dilling at Étretat. (Image used with permission from the *American Harp Journal*)

Epigraph. From Renié's meditation dated August 15, 1925.

vibrantly. Its sonority under the fingers of the artist was beautiful and exquisite."[54] After another concert, she received a review which complimented her artistry: "Power, virtuosity, style, charm. Henriette Renié possesses these qualities in their highest expression. She proclaimed them at her concert with a widely-varied program; her *Contemplation* and several transcriptions were encored with enthusiasm, and the evening was a continuous triumph for her. . . ."[55]

These reviews reveal the deep virtuosic undercurrent with which she infused her own compositions for harp. Few works in the modern harp's repertoire display such depth as *Légende, Ballade fantastique, Pièce symphonique, Danse des lutins* and her lesser-known *Deux promenades matinales.* No discussion of Renié's artistry of performance would be complete without mentioning these works, written by a virtuoso to be played only by masters of the harp. In each of these compositions, she shares a different aspect of her own stunning artistry: *Légende* in its use of thematic motives and textures to tell a devastating story; *Pièce symphonique* in its use of the harp as a full orchestra; *Danse des lutins** in its interwoven chromaticism; and *Deux promenades matinales* in their vivid depiction of her

---

* Mlle Renié based *Danse des lutins* upon a few lines of text by Sir Walter Scott from his poem entitled "The Lay of the Last Minstrel," depicting the joyful dancing of goblins: "See their agile feet, listen to their sweet music." The importance of this quote is not lost on any harpist who plays this work, which requires nearly 300 pedal changes to be made in only three minutes of music.

deep spirituality through a stroll amidst the cliffs of Étretat, France. Renié balances the varied colors of the harp is if she were writing for an orchestra; she blends nuances and timbres to create a vibrant setting. Like an expert storyteller, she holds the listeners' interest as they wonder how her story might unfold. The basis for each of these compositions revolves around strikingly different scenarios. Each is singular in achieving its own effect with the harp as its medium.

Légende

Written in 1901 and performed for the first time in 1902, *Légende* is perhaps the most recognized and performed work by Renié.[56] It is the first large work that she wrote for solo harp, and she performed it at nearly every concert when she toured with the Lamoureux Orchestra directed by Camille Chevillard.[57] Shortly after Mlle Renié began performing this work, which displayed the capabilities of the double-action harp, several composers were spurred to a renewed interest in writing for the instrument.[58]

Renié made an acclaimed recording of *Légende* on the Odéon label around 1926. The process of recording in that era was quite different from today. Works were recorded in a single "take," requiring the artist to play perfectly through the entire work with no stops. Furthermore, recordings were often selected, based not on the success of an artist's specific performance, but on the technical merit of the recording itself. For these reasons, she found the process of recording to be tremendously stressful and exhausting. Because the maximum length on each side of records was three minutes, her recording of *Légende* was split between two different sides of the record. The full work was therefore adjusted from nine minutes to six (with no cuts). Because the performance

---

Opposite: Henriette Renié, ca 1900. (Image used with permission from the *American Harp Journal*)

needed to be compressed to fit on the record and this compression wasn't evenly distributed, the result was a noticeable difference of several pitches between these two sides of the record.[59] Her Odéon recordings were sold out within six months of their release and she subsequently received many enticing offers, but refused to record again until the technical quality of the recording system was improved.[60]

Légende is based on the poem "Les elfes" by Leconte de Lisle (1818–1894), a French poet of the Parnassian movement.[*] This composition blends Renié's dramatic sensitivity for the instrument with the Romantic influence in her writing and her love of literature and poetry. Her virtuosity is revealed through subtle compositional variation. This occurs in several ways, including the development of motives using the effects of timbre and range to translate the haunting tale by de Lisle into music. A translation of the poem follows.

"Les elfes" by Charles Marie Leconte de Lisle (1818–1894)
English Translation by Claire Renaud, edited by Jaymee Haefner

Crowned with Thyme and Marjoram,
Joyful elves dance on the plain

---

[*] This movement of French poets strove for the flawless craft of writing poems in perfect form, treated with emotional detachment. They followed the doctrine of Théopile Gautier, advocating "art for art's sake," which was a reaction against the loose poetic forms of that time.

From the woody trail to the familiar deer
On a black horse appeared a Knight
His golden spur shone in the dusky night
And when he passed in a ray of light
One could see, always changing,
On his locks a silver helmet gleaming

Crowned with Thyme and Marjoram,
Joyful elves dance on the plain

They all surrounded him like a light swarm
Which in the mute air seemed to flutter about
—Hail, bold Knight, in the peaceful night.
Where are you going so late, said the young queen.
Evil spirits haunt the forests
Come and dance rather on the fresh lawns

Crowned with Thyme and Marjoram,
Joyful elves dance on the plain

—No! My fiancée with bright and sweet eyes
Awaits me and tomorrow we will be married
Let me go, Elves of the plain,
Who dance in a round on the moss in bloom.
Do not delay me far from my love
As already the day breaks

Crowned with Thyme and Marjoram,
Joyful elves dance on the plain

—Stay knight. I will give you
The magic Opal and the golden ring.
And, something worth more than glory and fortune
My gown spun with moonlight beams.
—No! he said. And with her white finger,
She touched the trembling knight on the heart.

31

> *Crowned with Thyme and Marjoram,*
> *Joyful elves dance on the plain*

> *And under the spur the black horse hastened*
> *It galloped, it dashed and sped without rest*
> *But the knight shivered and bent himself*
> *He saw on the road a white shape*
> *Walking noiselessly its arms reaching towards him;*
> *—Elf, spirit, evil, do not stop me.*

> *Crowned with Thyme and Marjoram,*
> *Joyful elves dance on the plain*

> *—Do not stop me, heinous ghost!*
> *I am going to marry my sweet-eyed beloved.*
> *—O my dear husband, the eternal grave*
> *Will be our wedding bed, she said.*
> *I am dead! And seeing her so,*
> *Of sorrow and love he fell dead also.*

> *Crowned with Thyme and Marjoram,*
> *Joyful elves dance on the plain*

In this tale, a Cavalier rides through the forest on the way to meet his Beloved on the night before their wedding. In the forest, he is intercepted by a group of Elves, plus the Queen of the Elves, who tries to seduce him. He refuses, stating that he is on the way to meet his true love, which angers the Queen. She then casts a spell upon him. At last he escapes, running from the Queen and encounters a ghostlike form. Thinking that the form is a demon, he curses it. The form stops him and reveals that she is his Beloved. She says ". . . the eternal tomb

will be our wedding bed. I am dead!" Out of grief and love for her, he
too falls dead. Thus, de Lisle's devastating story of Love–Death is an
echo of the premise for Wagner's opera *Tristan und Isolde*.

Within this poem, a descriptive refrain about the Elves is repeated
seven times:

> Crowned with Thyme and Marjoram,
> Joyful elves dance on the plain

Many of the virtuosic elements portrayed by Renié in this work
can be seen by examining her seven settings of this refrain, each
with a unique treatment of the melody. The first appearance of
this refrain is heard in measure (m.) 23, immediately following
the introduction. In this work, Mlle Renié treats this refrain
as a variation, which is repeated and altered according to the
surrounding events of the poem. The melody is characterized by
a chromatic motive which falls by half steps and is repeated up a
third before falling again (Example 2.1).

Example 2.1: *Légende*, mm. 23–5.
(Publisher: Alphonse Leduc; reprinted by permission.)

This makes the motive sound circular and futile, representing the Cavalier's confusion created by the encounter with the Elves. The motive is rhythmically active, but the melody continuously circles around the same notes. In the early and late appearances of this refrain, the dotted rhythms exhibit the frantic gallop of the Cavalier's horse.

This heavily dotted variation of the refrain is then transferred up an octave in m. 39, and later with heavy triplets which radiate the Cavalier's growing desperation (Example 2.2). The triplet figure is particularly effective, for Renié uses repeated three-note chords in the right hand, alternating with octaves at the lowest range of the harp. These two lines create two distinct timbres on the harp, with the right hand playing the gut strings in the most resonant range of the harp near middle C, while the left hand plays the bass wire strings. One could easily imagine this passage orchestrated with contrabass striking the low left-hand octaves and a brass ensemble playing the upper right-hand line.

Example 2.2: *Légende*, mm. 53–4.
(Publisher: Alphonse Leduc; reprinted by permission.)

In contrast, the Elves' effect on this motive can be heard in m. 75, where the texture suddenly becomes light and airy as the elves dance around the Cavalier (Example 2.3). This is the first time in the work when the right and left hand both remain above middle C for an extended length of time. The motive is transformed to a light *bisbigliando* with alternating linear intervals repeated between the hands in opposite directions. This effect is particularly idiomatic to the harp, because the left and right hand approach the strings from opposite sides of the instrument, which requires quick replacement. Renié used a sudden change of register in this section to emphasize the textural shift.

Example 2.3: *Légende*, mm. 75–6.
(Publisher: Alphonse Leduc; reprinted by permission.)

One of the most effective techniques in this work occurs with the contrast created between highly technical sections and moments of clear melody in octaves. For example, a translucent melody frames the Elves' variation (Example 2.4). This motive in mm. 111–2 seems to ask, "Did you hear that?"

Example 2.4: *Légende*, mm. 111–3.
(Publisher: Alphonse Leduc; reprinted by permission.)

This moment of calm simplicity is short-lived however, as the listeners are soon enveloped by a sweetly contrasting style, revealed through lush chords in B♭ major as the Cavalier describes his Beloved to the Elves.

An example of dramatic range use can be seen in the introduction (mm. 1–22) and conclusion (mm. 255–72) of *Légende.* This work opens with an octave played on the lowest string of the harp (C). By m. 18, the melody has traveled seven octaves upwards to the highest strings of the harp. Few harp compositions of this time spanned such a broad range, especially within the first page of the composition. Moreover, this alternation between low and high range in the introduction culminates in a sweep of parallel tenths which step over one another from the very top of the harp back to the lowest C string before an explosive glissando back to the top of the harp (Example 2.5).

Example 2.5: *Légende,* **mm. 21–2.**
(Publisher: Alphonse Leduc; reprinted by permission.)

Renié uses subtle means for adjusting the specific timbre. One of the first instances of this is in the *bisbigliando* passage, previously discussed. Another instance occurs in m. 165 where two notes are alternated, using enharmonic doubling to play a repeating pitch with the second, third and fourth fingers (Example 2.6).

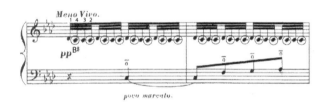

Example 2.6: *Légende,* **mm. 165–6. Enharmonic notation and fingering added by the author.**
(Publisher: Alphonse Leduc; reprinted by permission.)

The passage is particularly well-suited to the harp, because of the enharmonic possibilities created by doubling the pitches on adjacent strings.* Another textural shift occurs in m. 173, where the Queen attempts to seduce the Cavalier by mimicking his

---

* This technique was formerly employed by Félix Godefroid in his *Étude de concert* (op. 193), another particularly virtuosic showpiece for the harp.

previous description of his Beloved (Example 2.7). Now, the melody

occurs as the lowest note in a series of ascending arpeggios.

Example 2.7: *Légende,* mm. 173–4.
(Publisher: Alphonse Leduc; reprinted by permission.)

Another effective timbre shift occurs in m. 229, where the

Cavalier is cursed by the Queen (Example 2.8). In this passage,

Renié asks the harpist to play with the nails, low on the strings to

create an ethereal timbre, which foreshadows the eerie encounter

with the Beloved's ghost.

Example 2.8: *Légende,* mm. 229–31.
(Publisher: Alphonse Leduc; reprinted by permission.)

These effects in *Légende* were created by a genius of the

harp, and this *tour de force* demands technical and interpretive virtuosity. It includes spectacular gestures which are most effective when navigated by an artist who is in absolute control throughout the performance. Clearly, Mlle Renié embodied this artistry, and she used the full range of the harp's timbres as an orchestra, achieving a display of great genius in this work.

Deux promenades matinales

Henriette Renié's *Deux promenades matinales* (Two Morning Walks) remain one of her most beautifully written works for harp—poetic and peaceful. Although these two movements are of a lighter subject than most of her other works, they require equally skilled interpretation. As a performer, Mlle Renié exemplified a balance between artistry and technique, so it is fitting that these traits are so prevalent in her own compositions.

She wrote her *Deux promenades matinales* in 1913, just before the start of World War I.[61] They evoke her experiences in Étretat, France, which is known for the views of its beautiful cliffs on the Normandy coast. Her family owned a villa there and she frequently visited it during the summer months. Specifically, her inspiration for these works came while she was standing on one of these cliffs overlooking the calm deep blue sea with the "glistening dew" on the cliffs above.[62] The work is composed in two sections, each displaying a very different scene from these Normandy cliffs.

The first *Matinale* is entitled *Au loin, dans la verdure, la mer calme et mystérieuse*, which translates to: "In the distance, in the greenery, the calm and mysterious sea..." This movement refers to a specific narrow valley in Étretat, where the blue, calm and mysterious sea emerges from a green nest; in the distance, a white

Opposite: Henriette Renié, ca 1900.

sail slowly rocks.[63] It relies more on depth of interpretation than technical flare, and one can witness the picturesque setting through her subtle use of development in this work through a four-part form of A A' B A".

The movement opens with a tempo marking of *andante*. The first two measures form a melodic arch which begins on and returns to an E♭ chord in first inversion followed by an echo of the same chord in the uppermost register of the harp (Example 2.9).

Example 2.9: *Deux promenades matinales,* **mvt. 1, mm. 1–4.**
(Publisher: Louis Rouhier; reprinted by permission from Alphonse Leduc.)

This opening motive sets the stage for the "calm and mysterious sea" (the lower chords) and the cliffs above (the upper arpeggiation). In common time ($\frac{4}{4}$ meter), it symbolizes the first steps on the Morning Walk, with the opening imagery as an anticipation of the walk's destination. This opening five-note motive, marked tenuto, represents "the walk," and becomes the basis for the left hand through the next nine measures. It is

developed into a triplet pattern during the repeat of the melody in
m. 15 (Example 2.10).

Example 2.10: *Deux promenades matinales*, **mvt. 1, mm. 15–6.**
(Publisher: Louis Rouhier; reprinted by permission from Alphonse Leduc.)

Likewise, the melody gains momentum as it is repeated one
octave higher. This movement is thus propelled as one climbs
the sides of the cliffs to reach the walk's destination. The five-
note motive of the walk remains constant throughout all three A
sections while the arpeggiated "imagery" around it is constantly
developed.

In contrast, the following section shifts abruptly to the tonality
of A minor, which is a tritone from the former tonality of E♭ major.
It represents the sail in the distance, which "slowly rocks." Framed
by two four-bar transitions, the melody in this section gradually
climbs chromatically back to E♭ major, the arrival of which adds to
the stunning brilliance of the following restatement of the theme
through expanded arpeggiated chords beginning in m. 50. This
setting represents the arrival at the cliffs of Étretat (Example 2.11).

Example 2.11: *Deux promenades matinales,* **mvt. 1, mm. 50–1.**
(Publisher: Louis Rouhier; reprinted by permission from Alphonse Leduc.)

The transition from minor back to the familiar major sound could be compared to a moment in the shadows of the cliffs, followed by the return to the warm sunlight and the dazzling view of the sea from the top of the cliffs of Étretat. This lovely melody within the last statement of the theme requires suppleness and mature interpretation to convey the serenity of the composition.

The second *Matinale,* entitled *Dans la campagne ensoleillée, la rosée scintilla* portrays an entirely different aspect of the Étretat cliffs. Its translation reads: "In the sunny countryside, the dew glistened. . . ." With over 250 pedal changes in four-and-a-half minutes, it requires technical virtuosity as opposed to the expressivity of interpretation shown by the first *Matinale.* It is more capricious in nature, yet charming, witty and whimsical. This movement emulates the immense countryside, which peacefully gleams with silent charm.[64]

The most striking difference between *Au loin* and *Dans la campagne* is the tempo; the first movement sets the scene of the Étretat cliffs in a calmly beautiful *andante*, whereas the second reveals the brilliance of the cliffs in *allegro*. The textures of these two movements are quite different. The first movement relies primarily on vertical chords and expanded arpeggios, while the main theme of the second movement is more percussive in nature, employing a much smaller melodic range. The second movement is more rhythmic, using offbeat hemiolas to punctuate its second theme, starting in m. 21 (Example 2.12).

Example 2.12: *Deux promenades matinales*, mvt. 2, mm. 21–4.
(Publisher: Louis Rouhier; reprinted by permission from Alphonse Leduc.)

These chords are framed by explosions of arpeggios which arch from the lowest to the highest areas of the harp's range. Coupled with these frequent rhythmic shifts are numerous tonal shifts, requiring the harpist to execute deft pedal changes. On the second page alone (mm. 21–44), eight different harmonic areas are visited in quick succession, each requiring two or more pedal movements.

The mood then abruptly changes to that of a *scherzando* in m. 45. This ushers in an entirely new theme, using four-note chords, alternated with enharmonic note repetitions.

In the middle section of this movement, the first theme is modified into an oscillating figure in F major, with the melody now appearing in the right hand rather than the left (Example 2.13).

Example 2.13: *Deux promenades matinales*, mvt. 2, mm. 61–4.
(Publisher: Louis Rouhier; reprinted by permission from Alphonse Leduc.)

After a brief *tranquillo* section in mm. 103–54, the movement builds up speed once more with a second variation on the first theme appearing in m. 179. The left hand again carries the melody in G major (Example 2.14).

Example 2.14: *Deux promenades matinales*, mvt. 2, mm. 179–80.
(Publisher: Louis Rouhier; reprinted by permission from Alphonse Leduc.)

This third section acts as a recapitulation, for the themes from the previous chordal hemiola and *scherzando* sections reappear. The surprise in this movement occurs in a short codetta section at m. 291, where a variation of the first theme from the first movement returns to join the themes of the second movement.

This work displays sudden shifts in texture and mood which are reminiscent of the grandest Romantic orchestral works, like those written by Liszt and Berlioz. During Renié's time, few works for harp contained these qualities since much of the harp's repertoire was saturated with salon-style nuances. The authentic colors of the harp now emerged, as the instrument indulged in a full spectrum of textures under Mlle Renié's skilled hands. Truly, the harp was waiting for a virtuoso-composer to heighten its potential through works such as these.

CHAPTER 3:
RENIÉ AS COMPOSER

It's very well written. You should do a lot more like that!

—Théodore Dubois

As a harpist in Paris at the start of the twentieth century, Mlle Renié had the unique opportunity to interact with some of the most influential composers of her time, including Gabriel Pierné, Claude Debussy, Maurice Ravel, Paul Dukas, Jules Massenet, Charles-Marie Widor and Théodore Dubois, to name just a few. Not only did she interact with these composers, she had a direct influence on several of their compositions, notably: *Fantaisie* (1905) by Théodore Dubois; *Choral et variations* (1909) by Charles-Marie Widor; and *Danse sacrée et danse profane* (1910) by Claude Debussy (which Renié arranged for pedal harp).[65] She premiered most of these works, as well as *Concertstück* (1903) by Gabriel Pierné and the less-known *Légende* by Philippe Gaubert (n.d.).[66] In one of her interviews, she mentioned working with Maurice Ravel before performing his *Introduction et allegro* (1905).[67] She was in the center of the musical world of the time, allowing her to promote

---

Opposite: Henriette Renié's harp studio at Rue de Passy, Paris (Image used with permission from the *American Harp Journal*)

Epigraph. Comment about Mlle Renié's first composition, *Andante religioso*.

the resources of the harp in Paris, one of the most important musical locales in the early twentieth century.

Renié's first compositions date from the time she studied at the Conservatoire de Paris with Charles Lenepveu and Théodore Dubois. She was reserved initially about sharing her compositions, perhaps because of being surrounded by eighteen men in her class. She later discussed two of her first compositions before a concert in 1946:

> It was a day in 1895 after an exam in the class of Counterpoint and Fugue when I composed the *Andante religioso*. The day before, I had presented a Fugue which was appreciated, and I had been reproached for not composing enough. The next day, I told myself: "They want me to compose? Well, then I will compose." I sat at my desk, and without much difficulty, I wrote the *Andante religioso* that you are going to hear. What was less easy was to show my composition. I was the only woman among a big class of men. At this time, the women did not compose. . . . For six weeks, I went to class with the piece in my briefcase without daring to show it to the Master. Finally, there was a day in the middle of Lent when only five or six of my comrades were in the class and there was not much work to show the Master, Théodore Dubois. I decided to take the piece out. Great interest from my comrades and the Master! While I was playing on the piano what I will play on the harp for you tonight, they half sung the violin part behind me. I still remember the exact words which Théodore Dubois said to me: "It's very

well written. You should do a lot more like that!"
Encouraged by this success, I immediately started the
Scherzo-Fantaisie, which took longer to finish, but
which obtained at least as much success. . . .[68]

Renié's next composition, *Contemplation*, remains one
of the most popular in the current harp repertoire. Though it
was the first harp solo she wrote, Renié later transcribed it
for harp sextet. Le Sextour de Harpes de Paris, founded by
Renié's student, Bertile Fournier, performed and recorded this
work later.[69] It was appropriately named, for it reveals the great
depths of her spirituality through its bittersweet sonorities. She
described "affection" as the impetus for this work.[70] The melody
came to her during her morning prayers while she visited the
château of Contenson.[71] During her stay, Renié gave lessons
to a young girl named Camille,* and Mlle Renié dedicated
Contemplation as a birthday present to Camille's mother, Mme.
Baronne de Rochetaillée.[72] Renié performed it for the first time
at the dedication of a chapel at the Contenson *château* on 15
August 1898.[73]

One of Renié's most notable compositions is her *Pièce
symphonique* which she began writing for the *concours* at the
Conservatoire de Paris in 1907. She had been deeply moved by the

---

* Mme. de Rochetaillée's daughter later became Mme. Broglié, who was a very
famous Baroness at that time.

death of one of her cousins who was her age. As Renié developed a melody for this work, she could only imagine a funeral march. Because of this she cancelled the submission of this work for the *concours*.[74] She based the three episodes (movements) of this work upon an epigraph which she wrote: "The thought of future hope does not destroy the sorrow, it transfigures it."[75] She describes the three sections as: (1) funeral march and deep pain, (2) the denial of the pain and the revolt through which the first ray of relief appears, and (3) the transfiguration of the pain and the triumph of the soul. *Pièce symphonique* is regarded by many of Renié's colleagues and students as her most profound and finest composition.[76]

Every year Mlle Renié would devote the month of July to composing and would search her soul for the melodies to share on her instrument.[77] She spent a great amount of time reading; therefore, many of her compositions take the form of narratives in which the harpist must simultaneously command the roles of concert artist and narrator. She adored the theater and drama, so her compositions naturally reflected these literary interests.[78] At the heart of many compositions by Renié are dark tales: Leconte de Lisle's poem "Les elfes" in *Légende* and Edgar Allan Poe's "Tell-Tale Heart" in *Ballade fantastique,* for example. Both works thereby take the form of Romantic program music.

Other works by Renié are more subtle in their literary influence; *Danse des lutins* was based on a bit of text by Sir Walter Scott. One can clearly witness the active, learned, imaginative mind of Renié and her natural gift for storytelling. She used music as her medium for dark tales, yet never stepped into the realm of avant-garde effects. To perform her works successfully, harpists must be willing to immerse themselves into the ethereal worlds that she crafts through sonorities and subtle effects. The influence of literature can be heard in Renié's earlier compositions, but it is more esoteric than the aforementioned programmatic works.

One of the greatest successes of her composing career is *Concerto en ut mineur*, which she began writing shortly after she completed her *Scherzo-Fantaisie* during her Conservatoire de Paris studies. While these two compositions reveal some of her most brilliant work, neither of these works rival the popularity of her *Légende*.

Concerto en ut mineur

March 24, 1901 was perhaps the most momentous day for Mlle Renié as a composer-performer, when she performed her *Concerto en ut mineur* (Concerto in C Minor) with Camille Chevillard and the *Orchestre des Concerts Lamoureux* (also called Concerts Lamoureux).[79] That evening also represented a victory for the establishment of the harp, for it was heard for the first time as a solo instrument in the acclaimed Great Sunday Concerts of Paris.[*] After its premier, Renié's Concerto was later used for the Conservatoire de Paris *concours* in 1905.[80] Following the success of this concerto, she wrote two more pieces for harp with orchestra, entitled *Deux pièces symphoniques: Elégie et Danse caprice,* which premiered in 1906 and 1907. Although these works did not enjoy the same fame as her *Concerto en ut mineur*, they did receive radiant reviews, especially for Renié's artistic "blend of sonorities" between the harp and orchestra.[81]

Renié began writing the first two movements of her *Concerto en ut mineur* when she was nearly twenty and studying composition at the Conservatoire de Paris.[82] She shared it with her former

---

Opposite: Henriette Renié is seated next to Théodore Dubois as a member of his composition class in 1895. During the same year, Renié shared her first composition, *Andante Religioso*, with her classmates.

[*] In the late nineteenth century, the Concerts Lamoureux became increasingly popular, eventually attaining audiences of two or three thousand for their great Sunday concerts which occurred in twenty-four-week seasons.

teacher, Théodore Dubois when it was completed a few years later, and he urged her to show it to Camille Chevillard.[83] His demeanor was gruff in their first encounter and Mlle Renié believed that the meeting was a disaster, but they soon became lifelong friends.[84] In one of her interviews, Renié humorously described the first rehearsal of her Concerto with the Lamoureux Orchestra:

> [Chevillard] even seemed to admire my work a lot. But on the night of the concert, I made a small remark about a tempo to him. Maybe he was cross—I don't know. He briskly answered, "Your Concerto has a lot of tempo changes. There are very beautiful works which don't change tempo." What to answer! Fifteen minutes before playing, I really couldn't do much about this!
>
> That's when Monsieur Blondel, the friendly director of the Maison Érard, came to tell me sweetly: "Well! It seems that Chevillard is really pleased!"
>
> "He doesn't seem like it!" I answered while turning on my heels. I left the poor Mister Blondel completely shocked.[85]

Despite this unsavory beginning, her performance was a tremendous success and lead to her association with Chevillard's esteemed colleagues. Through Chevillard, she subsequently mingled with some of the most famous musicians and composers of Paris.

One of Renié's favorite composers was César Franck and the influence of his compositional style can be observed in her

Concerto, especially in the superposition of themes in the first two movements. Her Concerto has a robust construction in four movements (*Allegro risoluto, Adagio, Scherzo* and *Allegro con fuoco*) which are very Romantic in influence.

The first movement (*Allegro risoluto*) is entwined by three themes. The first of these is introduced by the orchestra at the opening (Example 3.1).

Example 3.1: *Concerto en ut mineur*, **mvt. 1, mm. 1–3 (piano reduction).**
(Publisher: Alphonse Leduc; reprinted by permission.)

The harp's entrance is then layered upon this theme in m. 17, with heavily dotted rhythms which are reminiscent of Richard Strauss in their grandness (Example 3.2).

Example 3.2: *Concerto en ut mineur*, **mvt. 1, m. 17–8 (harp).**
(Publisher: Alphonse Leduc; reprinted by permission.)

At the *poco meno vivo* in m. 80, the dark clouds of C minor part, and the oboe emerges for a moment in the key of G minor with a backdrop of harp glissandi, giving this third theme a waltz-like sentimentality (Example 3.3).

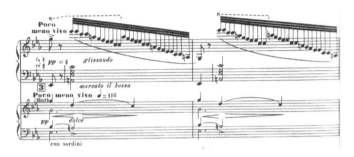

Example 3.3: *Concerto en ut mineur*, mvt. 1, mm.
82–3 (harp and piano reduction).
(Publisher: Alphonse Leduc; reprinted with permission.)

Suddenly, the listeners are bounced back to the opening theme in the key of B♭ minor in m. 90. The transition, which begins at the *poco più mosso* in m. 112, explores the first theme without the dotted rhythm and modulates to several keys, opening into a brief cadenza with trills and harmonics in the left hand. The remainder of the movement continues to mix and layer the sweet melody of the third theme with the darker first two themes. The movement culminates with an energetic *presto*, using the first two themes in m. 309, bringing it to a brilliant and virtuosic close.

The second movement (*Adagio*) shows the serenely spiritual aspect of Renié's compositional style and acts as a loving dialogue

between the harp and orchestra. In a three-part form, it is more
chromatic than the first movement; the chromaticism, however,
often occurs at the end of melodic phrases which allows the melody
to travel upward and arch downward toward its starting point. This
movement is based on four principal themes in which Renié reveals
her creativity in melodic layering. The first is introduced by the
harp, heard alone in the opening four measures (Example 3.4). The
orchestra then replies by repeating this melody back to the harp.

Example 3.4: *Concerto en ut mineur*, mvt. 2, mm. 1–4 with pickup (harp).
(Publisher: Alphonse Leduc; reprinted by permission.)

A development of this theme is introduced by the harp in m. 17
(Example 3.5, *Un poco meno lento*), which expounds on the sonorous
leap and stepwise fall that occurred midway through the first theme.

Example 3.5: *Concerto en ut mineur*, mvt. 2, mm. 17–9 with pickup (harp).
(Publisher: Alphonse Leduc; reprinted by permission.)

The middle section of this movement is distinguished by its use of the triplet in the accompaniment of the left hand in the second theme. It is then transferred to the F minor melody in the orchestra to create an entirely new theme in m. 36 (Example 3.6, *Un poco più lento*).

Example 3.6: *Concerto en ut mineur*, mvt. 2, mm. 36–7 (piano reduction).
(Publisher: Alphonse Leduc; reprinted by permission.)

This theme retains the melodic motive of the falling fourth which was initially heard in mm. 17–8 between D♭ and A♭. This falling fourth now occurs in mm. 36–7 between the start of the phrase on F and the end of the phrase on C. Another related theme which displays the downward melodic shape is introduced by the harp in m. 52 (Example 3.7, *Largamente*).

Example 3.7: *Concerto en ut mineur*, **mvt. 2, mm. 52–3 (harp).**
(Publisher: Alphonse Leduc; reprinted by permission.)

These third and fourth themes are then superimposed upon one another in mm. 66–9 (Example 3.8).

Example 3.8: *Concerto en ut mineur*, **mvt. 2, mm.**
66–7 (harp and piano reduction).
(Publisher: Alphonse Leduc; reprinted by permission.)

The most dramatic moment of the movement occurs with the return of the opening material in the original tempo in m. 76. This melodic material now is treated as a two-part fugue, followed by the first tutti treatment of this motive with harp and orchestra in mm. 80–1 and a tutti rest. In this way, the theme is superimposed upon itself.

The build to the climax begins in m. 86 (*Un poco meno vivo*), when the fourth theme from the middle section is played by the harpist in octaves against the second theme in the orchestra (Example 3.9).

Example 3.9: *Concerto en ut mineur*, **mvt. 2, mm. 86–7 (harp and piano reduction).**
(Publisher: Alphonse Leduc; reprinted by permission.)

Although this section sounds developmental, it provides the transition to an ethereal and contemplative ending which uses the third theme and left hand harmonics.

The third movement (*Scherzo*) is more loosely constructed in three parts, as a sonorous trio bounded by two *scherzos* which are quick and light. It is the most dancelike of the movements in the Concerto. The harp and orchestra frequently trade themes as in previous movements, but less layering of these themes occurs in this movement. This *scherzo* theme (Example 3.10) is taken directly from the second theme of the first movement.

Example 3.10: *Concerto en ut mineur*, mvt. 3, mm. 1–4 (harp).
Compare with Example 3.2 (*Concerto en ut mineur*, mvt. 1, m. 17).
(Publisher: Alphonse Leduc; reprinted by permission.)

The main theme from the trio section is unique (Example 3.11), while it is similar in shape to the themes from the center of the second movement.

Example 3.11: *Concerto en ut mineur*, mvt. 3, mm. 75–8 (harp).
(Publisher: Alphonse Leduc; reprinted by permission.)

The *scherzo* then returns, ending with a virtuosic *presto*, with the *scherzo* theme played by the orchestra to the end.[*]

The final movement (*Allegro con fuoco*) is marked by more harp solos than the other three movements and a return to a heavier quasi-Romantic style. This movement consists of two main themes, the first of which is introduced with the first harp solo in m. 5 (Example 3.12) after a brief orchestral introduction.

Example 3.12: *Concerto en ut mineur*, **mvt. 4, mm. 5–8 (harp).**
(Publisher: Alphonse Leduc; reprinted by permission.)

Like the first movement, this theme is heavily syncopated. The second theme occurs in m. 75 (Example 3.13, *Un peu moins vite*), introduced by the harp:

Example 3.13: *Concerto en ut mineur*, **mvt. 4, mm. 75–7 (harp).**
(Publisher: Alphonse Leduc; reprinted by permission.)

---

[*] Mlle Renié also included an optional section of music to connect the *Scherzo* with the *Final*.

This new theme marks the developmental middle section of this movement. It leads steadily through several new keys, but always toward the return of the main theme in C minor at m. 155. After this restatement, the harp triumphantly plays the main theme in E♭ major for the first time, after which several modulations on the second theme occur, eventually leading to C major. The movement closes victoriously with the main theme in C major.

A great part of the success enjoyed by Mlle Renié's Concerto came from the harp's audibility in front of the orchestra, which can be attributed solely to Renié's sensitivity to orchestrating around the harp's natural sonority. Throughout this Concerto, she reveals the potential of virtuosity on the harp, not only through her idiomatic writing, but through her careful balance of other instruments with the harp. Her inner vitality and the reflection of her love for this instrument may be found through her mastery of composition.

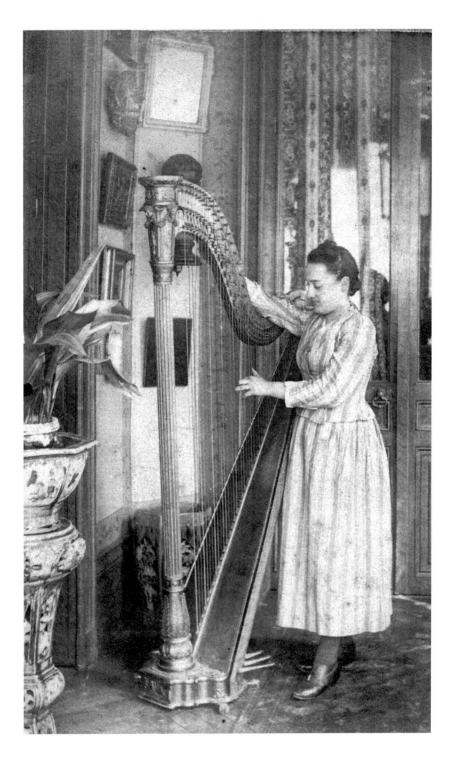

Scherzo-Fantaisie

Renié composed her *Scherzo-Fantaisie* for harp (or piano) and violin in 1895 during her compositional studies at the Conservatoire de Paris. She composed it just after finishing her *Andante religioso,* which was also written for harp and violin. While it is not as mature in stature as her later works such as *Pièce symphonique* (1907), *Deux promenades matinales* (1913), and even her *Concerto en ut mineur* (1901), her *Scherzo-Fantaisie* is an anticipation of the brilliance that would blossom in her later compositions. One can hear her love of dotted rhythms, which permeate many of her other compositions (*Pièce symphonique* and *Légende,* for example). Renié abandoned the practice of including an alternate piano staff after publishing this work, as the harp's identity continued to separate from the keyboard idiom during the turn of the century.

One of the earliest performances of her *Scherzo-Fantaisie* took place at *Salle Érard,* and in one of her pre-performance talks, Renié mentioned that it had gained a great amount of success with Xavier Leroux and Théodore Dubois.[86] This work primarily demonstrates the technical virtuosity of the harpist using chords and arpeggios within a strict three-part form. The work contains several student qualities. For example, she used double flats to notate accidentals which would often be written enharmonically to facilitate playing chromatic lines on the harp. She occasionally used this in other works, including *Légende*, but harpists often find this notation uncomfortable to read.

One aspect of this composition that sets it apart from many harp duets with other instruments is the attention that Renié paid to the individual sonorities of the violin and harp. Many violin and harp duets tend to showcase the virtuosity of the violin, whereas this work accentuates the resonance of the harp. The opening motive in A minor is an excellent example of her balance between the violin and harp. In these opening measures, the full chords and arpeggios of the harp perfectly counterbalance the brilliant register of the violin (Example 3.14)

Example 3.14: *Scherzo-Fantaisie*, mm. 1–3 with pickup.
(Publisher: Louis Rouhier; reprinted by permission from Alphonse Leduc)

One of Renié's most prominent compositional signatures may be heard in mm. 4–5, where she writes staccato octaves in the left hand, punctuated by chords in the upper register of the harp on the off-beats (Example 3.15).*

Example 3.15: *Scherzo-Fantaisie,* **mm. 4–5.**
(Publisher: Louis Rouhier; reprinted by permission from Alphonse Leduc)

The middle section of this work begins in m. 33 (*Un peu retenu*), marked by a lighter texture of harp glissandi which cross over the syncopated notes of the violin. While the angular rhythms of the violin are still present in this section, they are softened by the new texture created by the harp. This leads to an amorous section of F major triplet arpeggios in m. 41 (*Plus lent*). Throughout this section, the melody of the violin rests just above that played by the harp, often at the harmonious interval of a third or a sixth as if it were a halo above the melody (Example 3.16).

---

* This compositional signature is evident in her later works for solo harp, as in *Légende*, where a similar motive is used to display the frantic gallop of the distressed Cavalier.

Example 3.16: *Scherzo-Fantaisie*, **mm. 46–7.**
(Publisher: Louis Rouhier; reprinted by permission from Alphonse Leduc)

In this way, the work is constructed more as a solo than a duet, with the violin as the upper accessory for the melody, both in terms of rhythm and range.

After passing through several harmonic changes, this section culminates with one of the largest climaxes of the work on a B major chord (the secondary dominant of A minor) in m. 79, after which the melody quietly arches downward, preparing the return of the main theme in A minor in m. 93. This moment is somewhat predictable, but the return of the main theme benefits from its poignant contrast with the middle section. It culminates in a quiet but vibrant *presto* in m. 115, which brings back the motive of unsettled offbeat chords in the uppermost register of the harp. This figure leads to the final climax in the final two measures of the work which suddenly crescendo from *pianissimo* to *fortissimo* in the span of one bar in m. 123.

The *Scherzo-Fantaisie* is simpler in construction than some of Renié's more mature works, yet it exemplifies her quickly maturing compositional style, revealing the robust qualities of the harp. Additionally, her balance of the two sonorities is carefully constructed in this work, which foretells her expert handling of orchestration in her *Concerto en ut mineur* and her *Deux pieces symphoniques (Elégie et Danse caprice)*. She shared her passion for the harp not only through performance, but through her teaching of these works to her cherished students.

CHAPTER 4:
RENIÉ AS TEACHER

I not only work for myself, now. I work for those who are going to continue after me. For an artist, I believe that the hope of passing the torch onto other hands, far from saddening him or her, on the contrary gives peace and joy to his or her life!

—Henriette Renié

Few musicians have experienced a career as dazzling as Mlle Renié, who introduced the harp and its capabilities as a solo instrument through the performance of her *Concerto en ut mineur* at the Great Sunday Concerts in Paris. Despite being extremely busy with concert engagements, Renié remained steadfastly devoted to her students.

Renié surmounted the great disappointment of not receiving the Conservatoire de Paris professorship,* a position she was denied upon Hasselmans's death, based on the anti-clerical government's view of her religious and political beliefs. Though Hasselmans

---

Opposite: Henriette Renié, in her studio at Étretat, France. (Image used with permission from the *American Harp Journal*)

Epigraph. A quote from Renié's program notes on 12 May 1946.

* See also chapter one for a discussion of the reasons why Mlle Renié was not granted this professorship.

recommended her for the position, it was consequently offered to Marcel Tournier.[87] Monsieur Pierre Mercier of the Conservatoire wrote to Renié about Tournier's appointment, and Renié replied with a respectful and elegant letter which began, "You are full of kindness, my dear Pierre. I thank you for your kind letter." At the end of the letter, she mentions that "God does what He must do,"[88] evidence of the great strength and conviction that her faith played in her life. When faced with even the most difficult obstacles, she emanated unwavering grace.

Henriette Renié never held a formal teaching position, yet her acclaim echoed around the world through the success of her former students, and some of the finest harpists traveled great distances to work with her. One of her most famous students, Susann McDonald, traveled to France upon the suggestion of Mildred Dilling and Marie Ludwig. After training with Renié in Paris and Étretat, she continued her lessons with Renié while studying with Lily Laskine at the Conservatoire de Paris. Susann McDonald was the first American to receive the *premier prix* from the Conservatoire, and her description of Mlle Renié provides a special view into her artistry as a teacher:

> Her lessons were unforgettable, as was her personality. She was incredibly dynamic, with a

strong and forceful temperament, yet at the same time very gentle and loving to me in our work together. She always inspired me to achieve the highest ideals in music, a vision which I have hopefully continued with my own students throughout these many years.[89]

To further refine their technique, many of the *premier prix* harpists of the Conservatoire de Paris came to study with her *after* winning their prestigious prizes.[90] Her legacy continues through the tireless devotion which she ignited in her students. Thus, Renié's teaching is still alive in the harp community.

An Analysis of *Méthode complète de harpe*

One of the clearest ways to gain insight to Renié's masterful teaching is to examine her *Méthode complète de harpe* (*Complete Method for Harp*), which she wrote during World War II (1939–1945). Renié expanded the scope of previous harp methods in the breadth and depth of topics she discussed. Her writing was particularly effective due to her three-fold expertise as virtuoso, composer and teacher.

Before Renié's time, several methods were written for the pedal harp in the eighteenth and nineteenth centuries. Respected harpists, including Meyer/Mayer (1732–1819), Krumpholtz (1745–1790), Cousineau (1753–1824), Désargus (1767–1832), Naderman (1773–1824), Dizi (1780–1835), Bochsa (1785–1856), Labarre (1805–1870), Lorenzi (1846–1922) and Grossi (1886–?) contributed with their methods.[91] Several of these harpists would have been in the middle of their careers when the double-action harp was created by Érard in 1810, after which a flurry of methods were written to help establish this new instrument. Renié's teacher, Alphonse Hasselmans (1845–1912) who essentially founded the French harp technique, may have been working on a harp method which was never published, based on papers that were found on his desk after his death.

Opposite: Henriette Renié, 1943. Photo for the publication of her *Méthode complète de harpe*. (Image used with permission from the *American Harp Journal*)

In 1943, Alphonse Leduc commissioned Renié to write her *Méthode complète de harpe* after the double-action harp had been established and flourished in France for over a century. Renié fully devoted herself to exploring the capabilities of the double-action harp and committing every nuance of her technique to paper. Rather than restricting herself to self-composed examples, she frequently referred to the compositions of others and she included these works in a detailed index at the end of each volume. Renié primarily used terminology which is directed at the already-accomplished teacher and harpist, rather than creating a self-directed guide to playing the harp for beginners. Her method stands apart from others in terms of its clarity, precision and scope of technique; these qualities, when combined with Renié's expertise as a teacher and performer, resulted in a harp method which is invaluable to harpists of any generation. In a letter discussing her method, Carlos Salzedo commented that it was "a gigantic work, and deeply captivating." He wrote that he wished that "nothing would stop the marvelous momentum of [her] devotion."[92]

Renié's method is comprised of two volumes: (1) *Technique* and (2) *Syntax*. The first volume (*Technique*) is divided into twelve lessons which teach the fundamentals of harp playing. Teachers should carefully consider that a student may need to take a great amount of time to progress from one lesson to the next, for these lessons are not intended to be "weekly" lessons for the beginning harpist. Each lesson covers several aspects of playing, and many of these lessons use the following format: (1) introduction of new technique(s) with illustrations and discussion, (2) exercises pertaining to the specific technique, and (3) a short piece which employs the new technique. Additional exercises for the seventh through twelfth lessons appear at the end of the volume, including three- and four-finger exercises which emphasize proper finger placement on the strings.

The second volume (*Syntax*) is organized by the discussion of specific techniques and effects, such as *étouffés,* articulations, harmonics and others. Renié offers specific advice on practicing for the skilled harpist, tips for repairing the harp, and transcriptions of harp parts from some of the most demanding orchestral works. The second volume is primarily directed at the established, experienced harpist and Renié wrote as if she were speaking with a colleague, rather than a harp novice. Renié included an extensive set of "Daily Exercises for the Articulation and the Independence of the Hands," which displays four-finger patterns in varied rhythmic combinations to strengthen the freedom of the hands and fingers.

The basis of Renié's technique can be summed up by the word "suppleness," explained in the Foreword. Suppleness allows harpists to perform technical passages with ease; in contrast, tension hinders technique. Above all, Renié believed this to be the most important aspect of a harpist's technique. She also discusses the need for pupils to *"love* the harp."[93] This idea is paramount, for it serves as the foundation of her instruction.

Renié opens the first volume (*Technique*) by explaining the basics of tuning, position of the instrument, and the hand and arm position. She included an illustration of the position of the instrument on the right shoulder of the harpist. She devotes an entire page to the important explanation that students should look at the strings "face on" rather than twisting their neck to the left side of the harp to see the strings from the side. This is a point not discussed in most harp methods. In her illustration, the right knee clearly makes contact with the back body of the harp, but the left knee is kept free of the instrument. This is quite different from Salzedo's method, which requires both knees to be in contact with the back of the instrument.[94]

Following these preliminary explanations, Renié begins a four-note exercise that requires the student to place all four fingers on the harp at once and play the strings individually. These exercises begin at a level aimed at new harpists who are already familiar with basic technique and reading music; the exercises progress rapidly through three-note arpeggios, the fingering of various intervals, rolled chords, and four-note groupings.

Renié frequently includes detailed aspects of harp technique. One explanation that sets her method apart is her discussion of sliding vertically on the string with the thumb or fourth finger while playing scales to retain the hand position in the center of the strings.[95] Though this is a technique that many harpists develop naturally to maintain a good tone, Renié was one of the first harpists to include it specifically in her method.

Several aspects of Renié's technique are very different from other popular harp methods. Perhaps the most important difference is the placement of the right-hand wrist. Renié writes: "As for the right hand, the wrist is placed on the side or entirely on the edge of the sounding board, according to the position of the arm."[96] This stands in sharp contrast to Salzedo's discussion of the same topic: ". . . the wrists (right as well as left) should not rest on the sounding board." Salzedo mentions that the wrists may occasionally touch the soundboard, but the right forearm "must be *absolutely horizontal*."[97] In contrast, Renié notes that a lowered right forearm may be helpful "in passages where the hand is not going or coming on the strings." Renié's discussion of this point agrees with Bochsa, who writes: "The right arm must be held in a sufficiently elevated manner, to place the hand in a downward position; in addition, the wrist of this arm rests upon the right edge of the sounding-board."[98] Clearly, several different perspectives have emerged, even though

Renié and Salzedo were both students of Alphonse Hasselmans at the Conservatoire de Paris.

Renié's explanation of harmonics is especially clear. She illustrates that right-hand harmonics should be formed on the space between the first and second joints of the index finger to "bridge" the string. Similarly, with the left hand, the fleshy area of the hand on the palm's pinky-side is used as the "bridge." Renié does not specifically explain the left hand "bridge" in words, but her illustration clearly shows this part of the hand in contact with the string.[99] She goes into greater detail with examples of harmonics in harp literature in the second volume of her method.[100]

As previously mentioned, Renié includes a great number of excerpts and works by other composers in her method. This is a particularly distinctive trait, for virtually all other harp methods contain only author-composed works and exercises. Renié's method is strengthened by interspersing new techniques and fresh styles throughout. Examples cited in her method include works by harpist-composers such as Zabel, Tournier, Bochsa and Hasselmans, as well as works by non-harpists like Debussy, Prokofiev and Granados. Paying tribute to these other composers in her own work is evidence of Renié's benevolent personality. She also included many excerpts of works by Tournier, who succeeded Hasselmans as the harp teacher at the Conservatoire de Paris.

These excerpts and compositions are presented at the same time as the techniques they display. Many other methods, such as the Salzedo/Lawrence method and that by Bochsa/Oberthür, contain large sections of prose, followed by exercises and compositions. Renié's organizational scheme, in contrast, helps to strengthen her explanations of specific techniques and effects by offering the pieces simultaneously.

Renié explains in the introduction that the second volume (*Syntax*) is directed at those who already know how to play the harp. She addresses the differences between the "old school" of harp playing "by Bochsa, Dizi, Labarre, Naderman and Parish Alvars" and the modern style of playing. She discusses the importance of the great classical works, which have opened many eras of music for the instrument via transcription.* Pedagogically, she felt that it was fundamentally important for students to experience and perform all styles of music. For this reason, Renié created her twelve volumes of transcriptions, which transferred exquisitely to the harp.

In the second volume of her method, Renié discusses works by non-harpists and various techniques that should be employed when playing these pieces. For example, she suggests an alternate

---

* Mlle Renié was responsible for creating one of the largest collection of harp transcriptions to date, entitled *Les classiques de la harpe* in twelve volumes.

pattern for the right hand in Prokofiev's Prelude no. 7 (from *Ten Piano Pieces,* op. 12) which is more idiomatic to the harp than the piano.[101] Renié gives a great amount of explanation to the difference between short, medium and long articulations and when each should be applied.[102] She discusses the finer points of performance, such as wrist movement, thumb placement and finger placement. These sections focus on specific exceptions to rules of technique. Renié suggests placing finger-by-finger in passages like her transcription of the *Adagio* by Beethoven (from Piano Sonata no. 14, op. 27, no. 2, "Moonlight").[103] Here, conventional placing rules do not apply because they would cause the strings to be dampened prematurely. She also discusses ways to avoid buzzing and special effects such as the quadruple glissandi in Ravel's *Introduction et allegro.*[104]

At the end of this second volume, Renié includes several challenging passages from orchestral repertoire. In these excerpts, she makes practical suggestions for orchestral harpists, such as enharmonic substitutions which make passages smoother (as in Chabrier's *España*), or re-fingering of difficult passages (such as the cadenza in Ravel's *Tziganne*). She offered multiple options for passages which are unidiomatic on the harp in their original form (such as the cadenza from Tchaikovsky's *Nutcracker*).

By combining her expertise in performance and pedagogy, Renié infused her *Méthode complète de harpe* with the same love of the harp that she instilled in her own students. Her method is still regarded as one of the most complete and valuable guides for harpists because it covers the execution of nearly every standard technique and offers ample examples from the repertoire. Renié approached the essence of harp playing both in breadth and in depth, qualities which far surpassed many other published harp methods. Renié continues to touch today's harpists with her deep passion for teaching the instrument.

Transcriptions for Harp *(Les classiques de la harpe)*

Along with establishing the harp as a solo instrument and creating some of the first landmark compositions for it, Mlle Renié made one of the largest contributions to harp repertoire through her twelve volumes of transcriptions for the harp, called *Les classiques de la harpe.* These transcriptions were a response to the growing need for pedagogical works of the Classical and early Romantic eras. Until the early nineteenth century, the harp had been essentially neglected by many composers because of its inferior tone and limited chromatic abilities. The capabilities of the harp improved with the invention of Érard's double-action harp in 1810, but by this time, the repertoire of the harp had already suffered. Serious harp students did not have any original repertoire from these eras to enrich their musical understanding. Renié created *Les classiques* out of her compelling belief that the study of such classics was fundamental to the musical development of students.

In one of her radio interviews aired by Radio-Sottens in 1965, she discussed the need for transcriptions in harp repertoire:

> INTERVIEWER: Does the public like transcriptions?
> RENIÉ: Yes; . . . I often have just as much success with transcriptions as with works written for the

---

Opposite: Henriette Renié in her garden at Rue de Passy, Paris during World War II. The windows were taped up in case of bombardment. (Image used with permission from the *American Harp Journal*)

> harp. Not only I, but all harpists play the *Arabesques* by Debussy, *Clair de lune,* and other transcribed works. . . .
> INTERVIEWER: By you?
> RENIÉ: By me.[105]

One of her most famous students, Marcel Grandjany, was even described as previously being envious of his friends, who played classics written by Couperin, Bach and Liszt on the piano. Grandjany, like Renié, found his way past this by creating numerous transcriptions for the harp.

The first ten volumes of *Les classiques* are generally progressive in difficulty, representing works which reach from Rameau to Liszt and Chopin,[*] with the last two volumes entirely devoted to works by J. S. Bach.[†] Several of the volumes are now out of print. Some works from *Les classiques,* such as Liszt's *Le rossignol* have now become standards in harp literature, even appearing on international harp competitions. Mlle Renié used these transcriptions in her recitals and performances, even including three in her recital of 1892.[106] The transcriptions she performed most frequently were: *First Arabesque* and *Clair de lune* by Debussy, *Au soir (Des Abends)* by Schumann,

---

[*] See Appendix B for a complete list of Mlle Renié's transcriptions and catalog numbers.

[†] According to Françoise des Varennes, each of the ten transcriptions of J. S. Bach's Preludes (Volume twelve of *Les classiques*) was dedicated to individual *premier prix* winners who studied with Renié after winning their prizes.

L'Egyptienne by Rameau, Menuet (HXVI: 6) by Haydn, Prelude

in C (op. 12, no. 7) by Prokofiev, *Tic-toc-choc ou les maillotins*

by Couperin and *Un sospiro* by Liszt.[107] Marcel Grandjany often

performed her transcription of Rameau's *L'Egyptienne*, alongside

her composition *Légende* and his own *Rhapsodie pour harpe.*[108]

On 11 January 1956, perhaps the last time her hands caressed the

strings of her dear harp, Renié gave a particularly memorable

performance of Liszt's Nocturne no. 3 (*Rêves d'amour*). Shortly

after this, she became ill and passed away.[109]

Mlle Renié worked on *Les classiques de la harpe* primarily

between the years of 1892 and 1923.[110] The twelve volumes

represent not only the single largest collection of harp

transcriptions to date, but some of the most carefully prepared

transcriptions for the instrument, especially in the careful

consideration of fingering and resonance. They are tangible

evidence of Renié's vast knowledge about repertoire of the

keyboard, for she was an accomplished pianist. She sometimes

needed to adjust the original material, and carefully prepared each

transcription to facilitate performance on the harp without marring

the conception of the composer.

In transcribing for harp one must contend with the fact that

harpists use only four fingers of each hand to play. Five-note

keyboard patterns can be particularly troubling, and Renié often included fingerings to make the passages more idiomatic and readable. For example, she carefully noted the left-hand fingering in her transcription of Beethoven's *Andante* from Piano Sonata no. 25, op. 79 (Example 4.1).

Example 4.1: Beethoven, *Andante* from Piano Sonata no. 25, op. 79 (from Renié's *Les classiques,* vol. 1), m. 16.
(Publisher: Alphonse Leduc; reprinted by permission.)

The fingering of the harpist's right hand is inverted compared to that which is used on the keyboard; on the harp, the right-hand thumb plays the highest notes, as opposed to the keyboard where the right-hand thumb plays the lowest notes. Thus, the finger spacing for *both* hands on the harp is like the left hand at the piano, with the thumb playing the highest notes.

Mlle Renié planned for the acoustic differences between the harp and the keyboard. By nature, the harp is an instrument on which each string resonates until muffled. The strings of the pianoforte, in comparison, are muffled as soon as the key is released. The extra notation of muffling* was often necessary to provide a clean sound on the harp and to preserve the original timbre of the composition. By notating the effect *bas dans les cordes* with a rippled line placed between the staves (Example 4.2), Renié achieved a similar effect without adding muffles. *Bas dans les cordes* indicates that the harpist should play low on the strings where the string is pulled taut. This produces a clean, refined sound on each string, much like that of a harpsichord or a guitar.

Example 4.2: Daquin, *L'hirondelle* (from Renié's *Les classiques*, vol. 2) mm. 16–8 with pickup.
(Publisher: Alphonse Leduc; reprinted by permission.)

Using the same string to play repeated notes can be problematic on the harp, due to the necessity of muffling that string when replacing the finger upon it. Harpists frequently double pitches enharmonically, so that more than one string can be used to repeat a note. One of the finest examples of enharmonic respelling can be seen in Renié's transcription of Mozart's Sonata in C

---

* Muffle (◔): Placing the hand or finger against the string(s) to dampen the sound.

(K545). Under the bass clef staff, Renié notates the enharmonic substitutions to be played, using *solfege* (Example 4.3).

**Example 4.3: Mozart, Sonata in C (K. 545), mvt. 1
(from Renié's *Les classiques,* vol. 4), mm. 14–5.**
(Publisher: Alphonse Leduc; reprinted by permission.)

Renié likewise treated Liszt's works with distinctive care. Many of his compositions contain figures such as arpeggios which are quite suited to the harp in their original form.[*] Many cadenzas in his works are playable on the harp with only a bit of enharmonic respelling. For example, Renié substitutes several enharmonic notes in the cadenza which occurs in m. 57 in *Un sospiro,* and she changes the sequenced falling figure to one more suited to the harp (compare the original version in Example 4.4 with Renié's transcription in Example 4.5).

---

[*] Some believe that this influence in Liszt's work came from his close friendship with the famous harpists Elias Parish Alvars (1808–1849), Rosalie Spohr (1829–1919), and Wilhelm Posse (1852–1925). He took harp lessons for a short time, but interestingly, he stopped his lessons because of the "pesky pedals." He frequently used passages in his works that are reminiscent of the harp's sonority, as well as explicit directions which inspire the tonality of the harp (*una corda* and *quasi arpa,* for example). See also: Dominique Piana, "Dolce quasi arpa: Franz Liszt and the Harp," *The American Harp Journal* 19 (Summer 2003): 8–11.

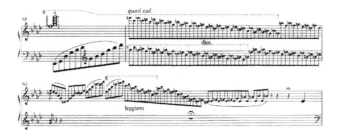

Example 4.4: Liszt, Nocturne no. 3, *des Rêves d'amour*
(from his *Neue Ausgabe sämtlicher Werke*), m. 57.
(Publisher: Alphonse Leduc; reprinted by permission.)

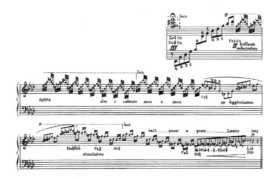

Example 4.5: Liszt, Nocturne no. 3, *des Rêves d'amour*
(from Renié's *Les classiques,* vol. 10), m. 57.
(Publisher: Alphonse Leduc; reprinted by permission.)

Renié considered the effect of certain keys upon the harp's natural resonance in her transcriptions. As discussed in chapter one, the pedal arrangements of the double-action harp change the length of each string by operating a fork mechanism which clasps each string. Just as a violin has its most resonant tone on open strings, the harp has its fullest tone when the fork mechanism is not engaged with the string, allowing the string to be as long as possible. The double-action harp sounds most resonant in keys which use flats or naturals, so Renié avoided keys with sharps whenever possible. She transposed Beethoven's *Adagio* from the "Moonlight Sonata" into C minor, rather than using the original key of C♯ minor. She ingeniously rewrote Chopin's Prelude no. 11 (op. 28) in the enharmonically equivalent key of C♭ major, instead of B major. Whenever possible, Renié used keys that were close or identical to the key of the original composition.

Despite Mlle Renié's extremely careful work in these transcriptions, one should note that the work labeled as Chopin's Prelude no. 2 (op. 28) in Volume 6 of *Les classiques* is actually Prelude no. 3, according to Chopin's thematic catalog by Maurice J. E. Brown.[111] Additionally, Rameau's Gavotte in Volume 7 is attributed to "Boréales," which, in fact is from his opera *Boréades*. Perhaps this error was a simple typo, given the limited resources available to Renié during the war-stricken time when she prepared these transcriptions; it is understandable that these errors could occur.

Henriette Renié made several transcriptions that were never published or were published separately from *Les classiques,* many of which are now out of print. Her transcriptions of *Habanera* by Emmanuel Chabrier, *Sorrente* by Théodore Dubois (from *20 pièces nouvelles de piano*), and two transcriptions from Isaac Albéniz: *Le printemps* and *L'automne* (from his *Album of Miniatures*), are no longer in circulation, and exist in only a few music libraries and personal collections.

She made countless unpublished transcriptions, and transcribed her own compositions, such as *Contemplation*, for her famous harp sextet.* This sextet was primarily comprised of harpists who had won the Conservatoire's *premier prix.* They frequently performed in Paris.[112] It was a great honor to perform as part of this sextet whose members included Suzanne Cotelle (the wife of Robert Blot, who conducted the Paris Opéra orchestra from 1946–1965) and Odette Le Dentu. One of Mlle Renié's pupils, Bertile Fournier, later founded Le Sextour de Harpes de Paris. This ensemble continued performing and recording Renié's transcriptions and compositions for six harps.

To closely examine Renié's method of transcription for solo harp, a detailed discussion of two transcriptions from *Les classiques* follows: *Tic-toc-choc ou les maillotins* by Couperin and *Moment musical* no. 3 by Schubert.

---

* A complete list of these transcriptions for harp sextet may be found in: Varennes, *Living Harp*, 133–137.

Tic-toc-choc ou les maillotins by François Couperin (1668–1733)

François Couperin's wrote more than 220 pieces for harpsichord, representing some of his finest work. His third book of pieces for the harpsichord (*Pièces de clavecin*) dates from 1722 and shows creativity in composition and includes whimsical titles for many pieces. In his first book, each *ordre** used traditional dance movement titles, but the subsequent books reflect ingenuity in each title. In the preface of his 1713 collection, Couperin discusses the source of creation for these distinctive titles:[113]

> In composing these pieces, I have always had an object† in view, furnished by various occasions. Thus the titles reflect my ideas; I may be forgiven for not explaining them all. However, since among these titles there are some which seem to flatter me, it would be as well to point out that the pieces which bear them are a kind of portrait which, under my fingers, have on occasion been found fair enough likenesses, and that the majority of these flattering titles are given to the amiable originals which I

---

* The term "ordre" was coined by Couperin to describe groups of pieces within each book which reflected the same tonality, and some semblance of mood, especially in his later books.

† Per David Fuller, the "object(s)" to which Couperin referred are persons "in high station." The last statement, then, is meant to keep him from being accused of "name-dropping." See also: David Fuller, "Of Portraits, 'Sapho' and Couperin: Titles and Characters in French Instrumental Music of the High Baroque," *Music & Letters* 78 (May 1997): 167.

wished to represent rather than to the copies which I took from them.

The title *Tic-toc-choc ou les maillotins* (an onomatopocia in French for the "hitting" or "clashing" sound of mallets) is particularly descriptive and appropriate for this work, featuring repeated sixteenth notes in the *rondeau* and each couplet. One can easily hear this percussive and melodious "impact" throughout the piece.

The original harpsichord version bears the inscription *"Pièce croisée,"* (literally, cross piece). This term was used by Couperin to describe works written for harpsichords with two manuals; the notes were written in close range with pitches which cross upon one another, frequently sounding unison pitches (Example 4.6).[114] He explains this term in the Preface of his *Troisième livre de pièces de clavecin* from 1722 and used this technique in only one composition before *Tic-toc-choc.*[115] The earlier instance appeared in his *Second livre de pièces de clavecin* and was entitled *Les bagatelles.*

Example 4.6: Couperin, *Tic-toc-choc ou les maillotins* **(from**
his *Œuvres complètes***), m. 1 with pickup measure.***
(Publisher: Éditions de l'Oiseau-Lyre; reprinted by permission.)

When notes are written in such close intervals, the harp has
a physical advantage over the modern single-manual keyboard
because the harpist's fingers approach the strings from opposite
sides of the instrument. Playing the same string simultaneously
with the left and right hands on the harp, however, would be
physically impossible. For this reason, Renié molded this work to
the harp by rewriting the treble line in the opening nine measures.
She substituted two-note chords for the single notes which
originally appeared on each offbeat, thus eliminating several
unison pitches (Example 4.7).

---

* The measure number references in this document begin with the first full
measure for examples from both Couperin's *Œuvres completes* and Renié's
transcription in *Les classiques*. The measure numbers differ between these two
editions because Couperin's *Œuvres completes* contains a written repeat of the
opening refrain, which appears between each couplet. Renié's transcription
does not contain a written repeat of the opening refrain.

Example 4.7: Couperin, *Tic-toc-choc ou les maillotins* (from Renié's *Les classiques*, vol. 6), m. 1 with pickup measure. Compare with Example 4.6 (Couperin's *Œuvres complètes*, m. 1 with pickup measure).
(Publisher: Alphonse Leduc; reprinted by permission.)

Renié's transcription of 1917[116] appears at first glance to be very different from the original, but the musical effect of the two versions is almost identical. In her transcription, the two hands play all the notes that existed in the original work, alternating rather than playing in tandem. To control the harp's resonance, Renié noted that the harpist should play using the technique *bas dans les cordes* (low on the strings) in several sections.

This work is in rondo form, indicated on the original harpsichord music (as *rondeau*). Composers in the seventeenth and eighteenth centuries frequently labeled the intermediate parts of the rondo form with the term "couplet." After each couplet, the opening refrain or "grand couplet" was to be repeated, though it was not often written out as such. This direction is not specifically marked in Mlle Renié's transcription; the couplets are clearly set off from one another by double bar lines, and one should note that the repeat sign at the bottom of the first page indicates a return to the opening, not a repeat of the individual couplet.

To facilitate the harp's resonance, Renié transposed the right-hand line one octave higher than its original placement, thereby avoiding the unison notes in the first and third couplets. This adjustment was suggested by Couperin in his Preface to *Troisième pièces de clavecin,* to facilitate the performance of this work on keyboards with only one manual.[117] In Renié's transcription, this creates a more-horizontal texture differing from that of the grand couplet. The second couplet again returns to the texture of the opening with the marking of *bas dans les cordes* (low on the strings). Two-note chords in the right hand rhythmically alternate with the melody in the left hand. Mlle Renié altered the texture slightly while she carefully preserved the notes and configuration of pitches of the original version. Near the end of the second couplet (m. 30), a descending scale in thirds occurs (Example 4.8). This passage may be played on the keyboard with two hands, but it requires precise fingering for the harpist because of the repeated string articulation.

Example 4.8: Couperin, *Tic-toc-choc ou les maillotins*,
(from his *Œuvres complètes*), m. 35.
(Publisher: Éditions de l'Oiseau-Lyre; reprinted by permission.)

Renié preserves the original pitches in this passage and notes that the harpist should slide the right-hand thumb along the top strings, while the second, third and fourth fingers of the right hand pluck the below notes (Example 4.9). This is a particularly effective technique on the harp, used for descending parallel intervals in quick succession.

Example 4.9: Couperin, *Tic-toc-choc ou les maillotins*
(from Renié's *Les classiques*, vol. 6), m. 27.
(Publisher: Alphonse Leduc; reprinted by permission.)

Another convention on the harp is to use enharmonically equivalent substitutions to avoid playing the same string twice in quick succession. This can be observed in the first couplet (m. 13), where "Si♯" is noted between the staves (Example 4.10). This indicates that the harpist should depress the B pedal to sharp, so that B♯ may be substituted for the first C♮ in the right hand, played with the fourth finger.

Example 4.10: Couperin, *Tic-toc-choc ou les maillotins*
(from Renié's *Les classiques*, vol. 6), m. 11.
(Publisher: Alphonse Leduc; reprinted by permission.)

The last refrain (grand couplet) in Mlle Renié's transcription then

reappears. After this refrain, the work concludes with a short

codetta with the right hand again transposed up one octave to allow

the right-hand melody to resonate without muffles.

The effect of this transcription is stunning, and one could

believe that it was originally written for the harp because of

Renié's conscientious treatment of the musical material. This work

has great value in the harp's repertoire, both as a pedagogical

work and a performance piece. In the span of only a few minutes,

it explores several technical challenges. Very few works for harp

are as exciting rhythmically and melodically. *Tic-toc-choc ou*

les maillotins became a crowning achievement for both François

Couperin and Henriette Renié, and is much-loved by audiences.

Moment musical no. 3 in F Minor, Op. 94 by Franz Schubert (1797–1828)

Franz Schubert composed his six *Moments musicaux,* Op. 94 (D. 780) between 1823 and 1828.[118] They represent the popular Romantic idiom of miniature self-contained works, and his third *Moment musical* remains the most popular from this collection. It is the only known work by Schubert that Mlle Renié transcribed. Originally, it was identified as *Air russe* (Russian Air) and it was included in a holiday collection of works entitled *Album musical,* published by Sauer & Leidesdorf. According to Robert Winters, this work "derives at least partly from its anticipation of a *pas seul** by Tchaikovsky."[119] In her transcription of this work for harp, Renié's careful attention and preservation of the original musical material is like that seen in her Baroque and Classical transcriptions in *Les classiques.*†

Renié's treatment of *Moment musical* no. 3 is noticeably different, compared with her transcriptional work in *Tic-toc-choc ou les maillotins.* Unlike that transcription which required a re-working of musical elements, she scarcely changed a note in

---

Opposite: Henriette Renié, 16 years old. (Image used with permission from the *American Harp Journal*)

* *pas seul:* a type of French solo dance.

† For example, see Renié's transcriptions of works by Bach (Volumes 11 and 12) and Mozart (Volume 4) in *Les classiques.*

Moment musical no. 3. The piece works quite well on the harp as written, but the genius of this transcription lies in Renié's noted fingerings and the sharing of notes between the left and right hands.

Mlle Renié made only one voicing change from the original work, which appears in the last chord, where she added a harmonic played by the left-hand thumb. This necessitated leaving out the C in the left-hand chord. The effect of this harmonic on the last note is brilliant, giving the last chord the quality of a bell. Together with the notation of *bas dans les cordes* in the preceding fifteen measures, this harmonic represents one of three elements which Renié added when transcribing this piece. The others are: the notation of fingering and exchanges of notes between the right and left hands; and notations of enharmonic equivalents.

Without Renié's clear fingering, several sections of this work would be perceived as unplayable on the harp. One example occurs in m. 4, where two grace notes precede the interval of a third in the right hand, with the bottom note repeated (Example 4.11). As previously discussed, quickly repeated notes can create buzzes and resonance problems on the harp. To avoid this, Renié indicated that the harpist should play the repeated A♭ string with the fourth finger and then the second finger. Although the string is still played twice in quick succession, the change of fingering alleviates the risk of buzzing and improves the sound quality.

**Example 4.11: Schubert, *Moment musical* no. 3
(from his Complete Works), mm. 3–4.**
(Publisher of reprint: Dover; reprinted by permission.)

**Example 4.12: Schubert, *Moment musical* no. 3 (from
Renié's *Les classiques*, vol. 3), mm. 3–4.**
(Publisher: Alphonse Leduc; reprinted by permission.)

In m. 3, Renié moved the notes of the last chord to the bass clef staff to give the right hand ample time to set up for the technical fingering in the fourth bar (Example 4.12). A similar notation occurs in m. 9, where the second chord of the measure appears in the left hand to facilitate the intricate right hand cross-fingering (compare the original version in Example 4.13 with Renié's transcription in Example 4.14).* In this measure, the right hand

---

* Cross-fingering on the harp refers to any passage where the fingers play out of their natural consecutive order (4-3-2-1 or 1-2-3-4). In this case, 4 and 2 are required to play together, followed by 1 and 3.

must first execute a thumb slide,* followed by quick cross-fingering

for the following thirds.

**Example 4.13: Schubert, *Moment musical* no. 3
(from his *Complete Works*), m. 9–10.**
(Publisher of reprint: Dover; reprinted by permission.)

**Example 4.14: Schubert, *Moment musical* no. 3 (from
Renié's *Les classiques*, vol. 6), m. 9–10.**
(Publisher: Alphonse Leduc; reprinted by permission.)

One should note that this passage of falling thirds includes five

notes, spanning from F up to C in the original score. Such passages

can be cumbersome to transcribe, since harpists play with only

---

* After plucking a harp string with the thumb, it normally closes completely
onto the side of the index finger. To play a thumb slide, a harpist leaves the
thumb in contact with the harp after plucking, so it passes to the next lower
note, rather than closing over the index finger.

four fingers. That is why this passage necessitates the use of the thumb slide and left hand chord.

Renié often included enharmonically equivalent pitches on the harp to improve the sonority. One of the clearest instances can be seen in m. 73 where she retained the pitches of the original score but noted "(SOL♭)" so the harpist would substitute G♭ for the F♯ written in the left hand (Example 4.15).* In this case, the G♭ has a more open sonority. More importantly, it avoids a pedal noise for the change of the accidental since the F string was played in natural (♮) position on the second eighth note of the measure.

Example 4.15: Schubert, *Moment musical* no. 3 (from Renié's *Les classiques*, vol. 6), m. 73–4.
(Publisher: Alphonse Leduc; reprinted by permission.)

Mlle Renié used enharmonic substitutions in other locations, writing the replacement pitches into the harp score rather than

---

* One should note that although G♭ and F♯ refer to the same keys on a keyboard, these refer to entirely different strings on the harp. The pitches sound the same, but G♭ refers to the G string in its longest state, and F♯ refers to the F string in its shortest state.

noting them as above. In m. 60, for example, a C♭ is noted as the lowest pitch in the left hand, though this is written as a B♮ for the keyboard. Simultaneously, a B♭ is to be played by the right hand. On the harp, it would be impossible to play a B♮ and a B♭ at the same time because each requires a specific setting of the B pedal, which can only be in the position of flat (♭), natural (♮), or sharp (♯). Renié rewrote the B♮ using an entirely different string on the harp (the C string). She employs many such rewritings in *Les classiques*.

Details such as these distinguish the transcriptions of expert harpists from those who are less adept at molding previously composed material for the instrument. Clearly, Renié was comfortable with the limitations of the harp and she transformed these limitations into acoustic advantages.

Pedagogical Repertoire

Renié enriched the pedagogical repertoire of the harp with many original compositions for her students. Several of her pieces fall into this category, including *Grand-mère raconte une histoire* (Grandmother Tells a Story); *Les pins de Charlannes* (The Pines of Charlannes); *Feuillets d'album* (Album Leaves); *Feuilles d'automne* (Autumn Leaves); *Six pièces* (Six Pieces), op.1 and *Six pièces brèves* (Six Short Pieces), op. 2. Fortunately, these works are all currently in print.

Two of these compositions, *Les pins de Charlannes* and *Grand-mère raconte une histoire,* are playable on the lever harp and are directed at beginning harp students. Mlle Renié composed *Les pins de Charlannes* in 1928,[120] and dedicated it to her goddaughter, Françoise Pignal (known as Françoise des Varennes). In this work, the first harp part includes clearly noted fingerings and the hands often double each other in octaves, which makes this an ideal work for a beginning harp student. The second harp (or piano), presumably to be played by the teacher, includes almost continuous eighth notes through the first section. This encourages the student to learn quarter-note subdivision. In the middle section, the first harp takes over the steady eighth notes, playing arched arpeggio

---

Opposite: Françoise des Varennes as a teenager and Henriette Renié, 1938. (Image used with permission from the *American Harp Journal*)

figures. Perhaps the most charming moment in this work comes in the last three measures, when the first harp plays a C major arpeggio from the top to the bottom of the harp while the second harp plays the same arpeggio in the opposite direction. Though this piece is simple, Renié enhances it through her natural nuance of expression.

Grand-mère raconte une histoire is a similarly charming, short work for non-pedal harp. She wrote it in 1926, and dedicated it to one of her small pupils, Francette Bacqueyrisse.[121] It is a slightly more difficult grade than *Les pins de Charlannes* and contains several important pedagogical elements, especially in the articulation of the left hand. In the opening line, the left hand is directed to use the fourth and second fingers with a break (**,**) between each note to continuously leave the string (or disconnect the placing) between each note. This motion in the left hand is superb for teaching a student the "suppleness" in the wrist described in Mlle Renié's method.[122] The frequent two-note chords of the right hand allow the student to practice playing intervals "from the bottom up," with the weight of the interval on the bottom note rather than the thumb.[123] Renié includes several nuances and dynamic markings in this short work, providing students with the opportunity to develop their musicality while enriching their technique.

Feuilles d'automne (Autumn Leaves) is an enchanting work which relies on the texture of large sonorous chords, especially in the low register of the harp. A quote by Victor Hugo* was the inspiration for this piece:

> Let us request: Here the night! The serious and serene night.
> All suffering and all complaints. Wearied nature,
> A time for sleep, a time for love.

Angélus, from *Feuillets d'album* is one of Renié's most-played pedagogical works. Written for a beginner on pedal harp, this piece was dedicated to one of her pupils, Mlle Urbainie de Terssac. The most striking aspect of this composition is Renié's use of enharmonics to achieve "bell tones" in the left hand at the beginning, and later to create grace notes of the same pitch in the right hand. This serves as an excellent introduction to this idiomatic harp technique.[†] The title of this work carries special meaning because in the Roman Catholic Church, "Angélus" is the term for a commemorative prayer for the Annunciation, accompanied by a bell call. Mlle Renié shared with one of her students, Sally Maxwell, that she specifically had the church on

---

[*] A well-respected nineteenth-century writer from France, Victor Hugo is especially known for his works *The Hunchback of Notre Dame* (1831) and *Les Misérable* (1862).

[†] For a brief discussion of the use of enharmonic notes on the harp, see "Renié's Influence on the History of the Harp" in chapter one.

the cliffs of Étretat in mind while writing this work. The opening

glissandi are meant to emulate the rolling waves hitting the cliffs

below the church. As one climbs the path to the church, the sound

of the waves becomes fainter, as the sounds of the bells (played by

the left hand) and the organ with choir (played by the right hand)

predominates. The piece ends with the sound of rolling glissandi

once again.[124]

Many of Renié's pedagogical works were composed late in

her career, when her life was more focused on teaching and the

creation of her *Méthode complète de harpe*. These works were

a clear response to a pedagogical need for repertoire that was

appropriate for her students. Their beauty emanates from her

artistic gift for writing poetic melodies, rather than the virtuosity

that can be heard in many of her more advanced compositions.

CHAPTER 5:
RENIÉ'S LEGACY

... The artist's soul ardently pursues an unattainable ideal; it has a passion for beauty which it can barely glimpse; it knows that the day it believes itself in possession of beauty, it will fade like a flower, since true Beauty is not attainable in this world; all one can try to do is to put oneself in such harmony with it that its rays can be reflected back and—perhaps shed light all about us.

—Henriette Renié

Though more than fifty years have passed since Mlle Renié walked upon this earth, her presence is still deeply felt in the world harp community. Her compositions are currently featured at harp competitions throughout the world, including the USA International Harp Competition, the International Harp Contest in Israel and the American Harp Society National Competition. Her students have continued to spread the knowledge of her technique and her passion for the instrument.

Despite the growing recognition of her influence, several of her compositions and transcriptions remain out of print and utterly

---

Opposite: Portrait painted by Gaetan de Navacelle, Renié at age 80. (Image used with permission from the *American Harp Journal*)

Epigraph. Varennes, *Living Harp,* 102. Mlle Renié wrote this in her meditations late in her life, after she had to cut *Ballade Fantastique* from a program due to her illness and exhaustion.

lost.* Her name is not even found in some of the most important musical reference books, for she did not make time to fill out the forms required for the inclusion in such books. Sadly, some of the information which is available in popular reference books (such as the *New Grove Dictionary of Music*) currently contain inaccuracies about Renié's career. The amount of literature about Renié's life and work is genuinely disproportionate to the deep imprint she made upon the harp's history and repertoire.

One might ask how this is possible, when Renié's impact on the history of the harp is unmistakable. One reason might be that her influence emerged during a time when few women were recognized for their achievements. While circumstances in her career were undoubtedly painful, she took these misfortunes gracefully, attributing them to the will of God.

Renié's spirit passed from this earth in 1956. Her enormous skill can still be heard through her recordings which are preserved at the International Harp Archives at Brigham Young University in Provo, Utah. One need only hear the opening notes of *Contemplation* or *Un sospiro* to understand that she exuded virtuosity with every touch of the strings. Her compositions remain

---

* Renié's compositions which are out of print include: *Scherzo-Fantaisie, Deuxième ballade, Deux pièces symphoniques,* and the Trio for harp, violin, and cello. Other works, such as *Fêtes enfantines* may exist only as unpublished manuscripts.

as a testament to her talent, for only a master of the harp could
conceive that such effects and nuances would be possible on the
instrument. Finally, her passion for teaching can be witnessed
through her *Méthode complète de harpe,* now respected throughout
the world. Her method and pedagogical compositions continue
to touch harpists everywhere—even those who have not had
the opportunity to study directly with one of her own students.
Now, Renié's students are publishing methods (such as *Harp for
Today* by Susann McDonald and Linda Wood Rollo), and Renié's
influence continues to shine though her students in them.

She stood only five feet tall, but Mlle Renié impact was truly
massive. Her endless devotion to the instrument raised the status
of the harp and its repertoire under the watchful eyes of the French
critics. Despite worldwide acclaim, she remained grounded by
those ideals which were most important in her life: religion and
family. One of the clearest examples of this came when she was
invited by Arturo Toscanini[*] to tour the United States. As soon as
she learned that she would not be able to easily return to France
if her mother became ill, she dropped the pen that she was using
to sign the contract.[125] She was endlessly devoted to her friends

---

[*] Arturo Toscanini (1867–1957) was conductor and artistic director of La
Scala (Milan), the Metropolitan Opera (New York City) and the New York
Philharmonic Orchestra. While at La Scala, he conducted the premières of *La
bohème* (Puccini) and *Pagliacci* (Leoncavallo).

such as Louise Regnier, her goddaughter Françoise des Varennes and her students. In the International Harp Archives, one can read countless tributes to Renié written upon her death by her close acquaintances, students and colleagues.

With these elements in mind, we might ask what can be done to strengthen and maintain Renié's legacy. One way might be with further research into her life and devotion and the impact she had on the musical climate during her lifetime. The two available biographies about her life, written by Françoise des Varennes and Odette de Montesquiou are insightful, but limited, tributes to her life. Another way is through the spread of her compositions. Several of her works such as *Légende* and *Contemplation* remain standards in the current repertoire of the harp, but one should hope that more of her compositions such as the *Deux promenades matinales*, *2ᵉ Ballade* and her Trio would enter the repertoire as standards. This could be facilitated by recordings such as those released by Susann McDonald (*A Tribute to Henriette Renié*) and Xavier de Maistre (*Henriette Renié*), which are solely devoted to her compositions. Projects like this have been in progress for many years. A collection of Renié's own performances were compiled on tape for the 1975 American Harp Society Conference by Sally Maxwell; this recording is now available on compact disc.[126] Combined with the inclusion of her works on international harp competitions, these are important steps on the path to making her music recognized by the public, which will potentially facilitate their reprinting.

The harp community has recently been spurred by a renewed interest in Henriette Renié. All the while, many aspects of this remarkable woman's life await discovery. After Mlle Renié's death, Françoise des Varennes traveled world-wide, sharing stories about this incomparable woman's life. After Françoise des Varennes's death in 2004, her mission was passed on to those harpists who have been touched by Renié's lifework and devotion. One of Renié's pupils, Marcel Grandjany, encouraged harpists to understand her "vibrant energy, her zest, and her virtuosity" by studying the *Allegro* from her Concerto and *Légende*.[127] Susann McDonald has devoted her teaching to Renié's vision, which is now pursued by her own students who teach throughout the world.

Indeed, Renié could have become a prodigy in any field she chose, for she was given intelligence and strength from birth which would have allowed her to succeed regardless of her vocation. Today's harpists are fortunate that she chose the harp as her profession, and we owe her much for her dedication to furthering the harp through her performing, composing and teaching.

The following set of interviews were aired by Radio-Sottens in August 1965 [possibly recorded in September 1955]. The original transcripts in French reside in the International Harp Archives at Brigham Young University (Henriette Renié and Françoise des Varennes papers, MSS 7778). These transcripts were translated by Claire Renaud and edited by Jaymee Haefner. A primary source for the book written by Françoise des Varennes about Renié's life (translated and published by Susann McDonald as Henriette Renié Living Harp*), these interviews center on Renié's work, as des Varennes worked tirelessly to preserve Renié's legacy in her own words.*

First Interview:

Introduction: The name Henriette Renié is forever linked with the harp. In honor of her eightieth birthday, the great artist, who was simultaneously an international virtuoso, professor and composer, agreed to ruminate on some memories of her incomparable career.

INTERVIEWER: Henriette Renié, what was your first encounter with the harp?

RENIÉ: It was in Nice, in a concert in which my father was singing and where I heard [Alphonse] Hasselmans. I was five-and-a-half years old; I was tiny, and I don't know what interior quivering must have moved my childish sensitivity, but in any

---

Opposite: Henriette Renié. Painting by her father, Jean-Émile Renié.

case, I told my father on the way back, "This man will be my harp teacher."

INTERVIEWER: With this decision?

RENIÉ: Yes, this decision. I was tiny. M[onsieur] Hasselmans was a 1.85 meters tall [just over six feet]. . .

INTERVIEWER: Were you already playing music at that time?

RENIÉ: Oh yes, I had started before the age of five, and I even played duets with my grandmother with such a remarkable rhythm that people would always say, "This little one will be a musician."

INTERVIEWER: Playing duets so young already indicates talent. When did you start the harp?

RENIÉ: I was musically gifted enough to start at about eight. However, I was very little, and for a year, I could only play exercises or very little pieces of two lines because I couldn't reach the pedals.

INTERVIEWER: It didn't disgust you?

RENIÉ: Oh no. Not at all! My enthusiasm stayed the same, I put the piano in second place and I victoriously put my harp first while working for two hours at my harp and a half hour at my piano!

INTERVIEWER: The dedication remained! Did your parents want you to pursue the career of a virtuoso?

RENIÉ: Oh no. Not at all! When I was nine, it was Hasselmans who was appointed at the Conservatoire in the middle of my first year, and he asked my father to put me in his class.

INTERVIEWER: Could you finally reach the pedals at that time?

RENIÉ: No; I was nine and I would still sit on a bench from which I would painfully come down to move a pedal on the right or on the left. I would then go back up on the bench, without letting go of my harp. Although this gymnastic move might have been funny for others, it wasn't easy for me.

INTERVIEWER: It must have seemed like a circus trick, right?

RENIÉ: Exactly, so much that my father had the great idea to create extensions in a mushroom shape that would clinch on to the pedals. With this, I managed to move all the pedals.

INTERVIEWER: So, from this moment on, you could play all the repertoire of the harp?

RENIÉ: Exactly—all the existing repertoire, which wasn't much.

INTERVIEWER: How old were you at your first competition?

RENIÉ: I was ten-and-a-half, let's say three-quarters.

INTERVIEWER: This wasn't old. What was your competition piece?

RENIÉ: The Parish Alvars Concerto.

INTERVIEWER: Were you aware of your talents?

RENIÉ: Not at all. I thought that all the others, being much older than I, must certainly have known more, in principle.

INTERVIEWER: Were you hoping for a reward anyways?

RENIÉ: Ah! Yes, I thought of receiving a second certificate, or maybe even the first certificate. When my father spoke of a *second prix,* I laughed at him and told him "Don't you think about it!" When he insisted, I said: "Listen. If I have a *second prix,* I'll make my fingers snap* in public!" I had four brothers! . . .

INTERVIEWER: Like that [*snap*].

RENIÉ: Ah! Yes, I don't know how to do it anymore, but at that time, I had four brothers with whom to play, and I was very boy like.

INTERVIEWER: Did you do it?

RENIÉ: Oh! I scrupulously kept my word!

INTERVIEWER: Fortunately, you had only promised to do this. What if you had promised to make a pirouette!

RENIÉ: It would have been a disaster. Can you imagine this, a somersault!

INTERVIEWER: All dignity would have been lost! You received your *premier prix* the following year?

RENIÉ: Yes, the following year and unanimously. I was so astonished by the enthusiastic effervescence in the room that I didn't think to wait for Ambroise Thomas to give me my prize, I was bowing while moving back, so much that an old porter came

---

* During Renié's time, snapping one's fingers in public was impolite.

to stop me with both of his hands while telling me: "So, you don't want to receive your *premier prix?!*" Then, I finally stood still.

INTERVIEWER: Were you expecting to get it?

RENIÉ: Yes, but I had a certain feeling. Most of all, I didn't expect to receive it alone, without my fellow student of the *second prix* from the previous year, who seemed old enough to be my father!

INTERVIEWER: You were still very short?

RENIÉ: Very short. By the way, I still had the extended pedals, and I was very childish. In the afternoon, instead of making myself seen at the piano competition, as the little prodigies often do, I stayed to play "old maid" with one of my little friends who was five. Every time someone brought a bouquet or congratulations, it would interrupt my game and it very much annoyed me!

INTERVIEWER: You must have received a good number of letters!

RENIÉ: Oh! A great many of them! It was very entertaining! There were several letters from very well-known and established artists. There were many articles. One of them, in *Le Figaro*, ended this way: "Ah! Little Renié, in the future, do not pull up your stockings in public, mademoiselle!" One must believe that I pulled up my stockings.

INTERVIEWER: Would it be indiscreet to ask you to let us hear the beginning of your competition piece?

RENIÉ: If you want. It was the *Concertino* by Oberthür. [*She played the first five measures.*]

INTERVIEWER: . . . Did you start giving lessons at a young age?

RENIÉ: At nine. My first year at the Conservatoire, I already had started to teach a young boy unhesitatingly. I was extremely severe, but this didn't prevent me from playing with him. One day, I started a new book of etudes. I was very proud you know; when one is small and that one starts a new book of etudes, it's a great joy. With despair, I saw that "For the use of beginners" was written on the front cover! I was so hurt that I covered my music before showing it to my student!

INTERVIEWER: What became of the student of the nine-year-old Henriette Renié?

RENIÉ: He made a good career as a harpist at the Opéra.[*]

INTERVIEWER: You were a teacher in your soul, almost from birth!

RENIÉ: Almost from birth. I loved it as much as playing.

INTERVIEWER: You started your career as a virtuoso very soon after your *premier prix?*

---

[*] This student was most likely Ferdinand Maignien. Many years later, he became the harpist for the Paris Opéra.

RENIÉ: Right away, two or three months later. I went to Queen Marie-Henriette of Belgium.

INTERVIEWER: She was especially interested in the harp?

RENIÉ: Yes. She herself was a student of Hasselmans. She was lovely; very simple and very nice. There was only one thing that perturbed me: she wore a small bonnet in lace. This was probably charming, but it made me think of the bonnet worn by an usherette. I didn't expect a crown, but still. . .

INTERVIEWER: One can easily imagine such a childish disappointment!

RENIÉ: Then I went to the Princess Mathilde, who was a lot more Imperialistic than her cousin Napoléon III. She was also very nice but seemed quite old to me.

INTERVIEWER: Of course, because you were very young!

RENIÉ: Naturally, I had played at many artists' homes: Pauline Viardot (sister of Malibran),* Diémer, who was in much demand, and. . . .

INTERVIEWER: The pianist?

---

* Pauline Viardot (1821–1910) was a respected mezzo-soprano in Paris. Maria Malibran (1808–1836) was one of the best-known opera virtuosos of the 19th century.

RENIÉ: Yes, the pianist Louis Diémer.* I had a profound admiration for him. He played the most difficult passages with such suppleness that I was captivated. This ease became my ambition. He was certainly a great influence in the suppleness that I acquired and in the ease of my technique.

INTERVIEWER: You understood the necessity of the complete mastery of technique, which thus allows the soul all the freedom of expression.

RENIÉ: This is exactly what I think and what I always say to my students!

INTERVIEWER: I'm very flattered!

RENIÉ: The technique is only used to express what one has in the heart without being bothered by the fingers.

INTERVIEWER: Yes, it's a means, not a goal.

RENIÉ: A means, but not a goal—exactly!

INTERVIEWER: Did composers take good care of the harp at that time?

RENIÉ: Not a bit. Nonetheless, in 1893, we obtained a piece by Saint-Saëns and another by Pierné in 1897. This *Impromptu-Caprice* is still very popular among harpists. Some pages are charming like this one. [*She played some measures.*] It was very

---

* Louis Diémer (1843–1919) was an acclaimed pianist and composer in France, known for his clarity and control in performances.

pretty but it didn't utilize all the resources of the instrument, modulations in particular. This is always the stumbling block for the harp.

INTERVIEWER: People such as Massenet and Gounod weren't interested?

RENIÉ: No, no one. I played the harp at Gounod's home. To finish, I even played a Fantaisie on *Faust* for him!* . . . I get red with embarrassment while thinking about that!

INTERVIEWER: It was some kind of arrangement?

RENIÉ: Exactly! I don't know how I dared to play that for him!

INTERVIEWER: Basically, he must have been very touched, since he was used to hearing all the barrel-organs play *Faust* on the street-corners (without meaning to offend you)!

INTERVIEWER: Despite this busy life, you continued with your musical studies after your *premier prix*?

RENIÉ: I completed my certificate of harmony, my harmony class, my certificate of counterpoint, then the fugue and composition class.

INTERVIEWER: Did you compose right away or did you only study?

RENIÉ: I started by studying. You know, there weren't any women who composed, except for Augusta Holmès and Cécile

---

* This *Fantaisie* was arranged by Albert Zabel (1834–1910).

Chaminade, and I was afraid to set myself apart; it intimidated me. Amid those eighteen young students, I was the only girl! All the same, I finally started to write a bit in my second year. I wrote some pieces for harp and violin, some melodies, and I mainly worked on the first two movements of my Concerto, which would later play a major role in my life.

INTERVIEWER: Your *Concerto en ut mineur*?

RENIÉ: Yes.

INTERVIEWER: It's this one that you started in the class?

RENIÉ: Yes, exactly. The second movement is identical. I didn't change a note in the orchestra parts or in the rest.

INTERVIEWER: How old were you then?

RENIÉ: I was . . . not quite twenty; it was sixty years ago.

INTERVIEWER: Did you change the first movement?

RENIÉ: Yes, the first movement. I altered it and developed it quite a bit.

INTERVIEWER: Since you agreed to play the harp earlier, would it be possible for us to hear the theme of the first movement of this Concerto?

RENIÉ: Just the first measures, which made Chevillard happy. He pretended that after that, one would become familiar. It's an *Allegro risoluto. [She played the first measures of her Concerto.]*

INTERVIEWER: It's very "risoluto" indeed!

RENIÉ: I was very determined and very energetic! The cousin of one of my students said that this beginning was a good representation of my lively and energetic personality.

INTERVIEWER: I believe that if your work glitters with life, it is also rich with sensitivity. To have a more complete idea of your Concerto, could we end by hearing the start of this *Adagio,* which you haven't altered since your class?

RENIÉ: If it pleases you.

[*End of the first interview with her playing the* Adagio *from her Concerto.*]

Introduction: Henriette Renié has already shared her fairytale beginnings. The little harpist, who revealed the capabilities of her instrument, became a brilliant virtuoso, simultaneously having a career as a teacher and composer.

INTERVIEWER: Henriette Renié, what was the most important event in your career?

RENIÉ: Without question, it was when I played my Concerto at Lamoureux. It was the first time that the harp was featured at the Great Concerts. Not only do I hold great gratitude for Chevillard, but I believe that all harpists should be grateful to him, since he took this responsibility upon himself. After its inclusion in the Great Concerts, the harp has been played in all the great symphonic concerts throughout the world.

INTERVIEWER: Until that point the harp had never been a solo instrument orchestra accompaniment?

RENIÉ: Never in the Great Sunday Concerts of the symphony; it existed only as an instrument which gave color to the orchestra.

INTERVIEWER: How did Camille Chevillard know about this work?

RENIÉ: I had asked to meet with him, upon the suggestion of Théodore Dubois. I was quite intimidated—and I rarely am. Maybe I also intimidated him, but it didn't seem to go well.

INTERVIEWER: It seems that nothing is quite as intimidating as a shy person. How did the meeting go?

RENIÉ: I played my Concerto for him. I don't know if you realize how difficult it is to play the parts of both the orchestra and the harp on the piano. I was sweating blood. After the first movement, he said: "After?" I played the second. He said: "Good. After?" I played the third, and he said: "After?" After the fourth we talked about the number of instruments necessary and that was it.

INTERVIEWER: It doesn't sound very encouraging. Did you intend to ask him to have this work performed with the Concerts Lamoureux?

RENIÉ: Not at all. I planned to ask him to conduct a concert I was giving where I had my own audience.

INTERVIEWER: After this strange introduction, how were the rehearsals?

RENIÉ: There was only one, which went very well. He even seemed to admire my work a lot. But, on the night of the concert, I made a small remark about a tempo to him. Maybe he was cross—I don't know. He briskly answered, "Your Concerto has a lot of tempo changes. There are very beautiful works which don't change tempo." What to answer! Fifteen minutes before playing, I really couldn't do much about this! That's when Monsieur Blondel, the friendly director of Maison Érard, came to tell me sweetly: "Well! It seems that Chevillard is really pleased!" "He doesn't seem like it!" I answered while turning on my heels. I left the poor Mister Blondel completely shocked.

INTERVIEWER: Although he didn't seem like it at that time, the following events proved that he was very happy!

RENIÉ: Of course! When I came to see him to pay the instrumentalists, he appeared voluntarily and suddenly asked: "Do you want to come and play your Concerto at Lamoureux?" I was so shocked that I stammered: "Wouldn't you prefer the Reinecke Concerto?" Unshakeable, he retorted: "No, it's yours that I want!" After that, he teased me many times for having offered another's work when I was asked for mine!

INTERVIEWER: Henriette Renié, how old were you then?

RENIÉ: I had just turned twenty-five.

INTERVIEWER: How marvelous to have commanded the harp in the Great Concerts with one's own Concerto, and at the age of twenty-five! How did the critics review this performance?

RENIÉ: Very well! And I must admit that I was very afraid of the critics, since that year everyone was criticizing all the Concertos. The review was excellent, even the one by "L'ouvreuse," which was known to publish harsh critiques.

INTERVIEWER: What about your artistic relationship with Chevillard—did you maintain it after that concert?

RENIÉ: Oh—an artistic and friendly relationship! His wife, the daughter of Lamoureux, became my best friend; he also became my friend, despite our sixteen years of difference in age. Each Wednesday, I went to dinner at their home. We would talk about music and play duets. Every Sunday, I went to listen to his magnificent concerts. It was a marvelous experience for me, since he wasn't content with merely conducting the orchestra; he gave his body and soul, absorbed by his art, and he sought to give life to the work he was conducting without being concerned with the public.

INTERVIEWER: Yes, he was truly an animator, one who gives a soul to the orchestra. It's surprising how he is now forgotten!

RENIÉ: Don't speak to me about it; it's disgusting and unbelievable! . . .

INTERVIEWER: . . . You probably had an enormous circle of artists, since Camille Chevillard was at the center at that time?

RENIÉ: I believe so! There were gatherings of all the great artists, starting with Van Dyck, the great singer of Wagner, the admirable Heanne Raunay, the exquisite Claire Croiza, and so many more! And then, at Chatou, they had a property that came

140

from Lamoureux, and we entertained all the great artists there. At that property, there was a tennis court, and we would compete: Pablo Casals, Jacques Thibaut, Paul Paray, etc... and one can't forget Chevillard, who wasn't to be left behind. We went there as much for pleasure as for work.

INTERVIEWER: It's charming!

RENIÉ: Oh, yes! I hold a fond memory of Chatou! . . .

INTERVIEWER: . . . Henriette Renié, after this introduction, you continued to premiere other works for harp and orchestra?

RENIÉ: Of course, by 1912, I played all the first performances with orchestra: the Great Concerts of the Conservatoire, Lamoureux, [Édouard] Colonne, and in all the existing Societies. I recall an unpleasant incident with Colonne, when I premiered Pierné's *Concertstück*.

INTERVIEWER: Yes?

RENIÉ: The *andante* accelerates. It ends of course, quite fast and with much warmth. Colonne thought that I was getting carried away. He was holding me back, and it annoyed me. So with my foot, I started to do this: [*she tapped the tempo with her foot*]. This didn't please the great orchestra conductor. He said to me: "Mademoiselle, play your tempo; I'll follow you," (which wasn't true) "but I don't want you to mark the tempo with the foot." I was upset. Finally, Pierné smoothed things over in a diplomatic way, but I wasn't pleased with Colonne; I didn't like him very much.

INTERVIEWER: It tested your relationship! With all your achievements as a virtuoso and a teacher, did you continue composing?

RENIÉ: Of course, only less than I would have liked.

INTERVIEWER: You wrote a piece based on the poem by Leconte de Lisle entitled "Les elfes"?

RENIÉ: Yes, *Légende*. It's even played at the beginning of each of our interviews. It's the first piece I composed for solo harp.* I believe it revealed the richness and possibilities of the harp to composers, which were unexplored before that time (despite the beautiful *Fantaisie* by Saint-Saëns and the famous *Impromptu-Caprice* by Pierné). After *Légende,* other composers felt that they could take more liberty in writing for the harp.

INTERVIEWER: Who were the first?

RENIÉ: Gabriel Fauré, Galeotti, Vierne, Ravel. This is how I met Ravel, for he came to my home so that I work with him on his *Introduction et allegro* that we were to perform together. Tennis had already brought Galeotti and me together! What's curious is

---

* In this interview, Renié mentions that this was the first piece she composed for solo harp, but she was undoubtedly referring to this as the first "large-scale work" for solo harp, since her *Contemplation* was composed before *Légende*.

to think that perhaps I owe the chromatic harp for all the efforts I made to reaffirm the resources of my dear instrument!

INTERVIEWER: A negative thing can trigger a good one!

RENIÉ: Well, yes!

INTERVIEWER: What are your main compositions?

RENIÉ: *Deux pièces symphoniques* with orchestra (first performance at Lamoureux), a Trio for harp, violin and cello, which received the Prix de Musique de Chambre at the Institut de France; *Ballade fantastique,* based on a tale by Edgar Allan Poe; *Pièce symphonique* in three episodes...

INTERVIEWER: Based on the stages of grief, right?

RENIÉ: You know this? Well, yes! First there is the Funeral March; then Appassionat[a],[*] which portrays revolt; and Peace which penetrates the soul, hinted at by the work's inscription.

INTERVIEWER: What is this inscription?

RENIÉ: "The thought of future hope does not destroy the sorrow, it transfigures it."

INTERVIEWER: It's very beautiful; I thought I remembered this.

RENIÉ: Then, I also composed the *Deuxième ballade,* the *Danse des lutins*, the *Promenades matinales*, etc., etc.

INTERVIEWER: Some of those works must have been used as pieces for the competition at the Conservatoire?

---

[*] This section was originally labeled as "Apassianato" in the interview transcript.

RENIÉ: Yes, and several times the Concerto and *Légende*.

INTERVIEWER: Does the harp have the same possibilities as the piano?

RENIÉ: Oh no! It's a mistake to always compare these two instruments, each having its own individual capabilities. The piano has two pedals, one of which lengthens and amplifies the sound, and the other gives the sound a smooth softness. One must not forget the union of these two, which creates remarkable effects. It's obvious that pianists can't have the poetry of harmonic sounds, the variety of the glissando, the airy* effects, nor the direct contact with the string which, in my opinion, makes the harp a unique instrument.

INTERVIEWER: Yes, the harp is a unique instrument; Musset writes of the living harp, attached to the heart. These airy effects you mentioned—aren't they found in your *Danse des lutins?*

RENIÉ: Yes, it's true, but even more perhaps in a passage of my *Légende* which emulates the circle of the Elves.

INTERVIEWER: You toured, right?

RENIÉ: Yes, in France and abroad, but not long ones compared to those now organized. However, one of them left me with an interesting memory. We were playing the same program every evening for eight days in a little town in Burgundy. The concert

---

* Undoubtedly, Renié is referring to the *bisbigliando* effect on the harp.

was in a movie theater bleached with lime, with a welcoming podium and barely any backstage. It didn't seem to be a very inspiring space, and it's there that I played my *Légende*. It was apparently so moving that, when I left the stage, my partners on the tour told me that they were overcome with emotion.

INTERVIEWER: And this in the most unspeakable of rooms! What a mystery! For the virtuoso, there is a kind of indefinable and unforeseeable condition of grace. On what do you believe such an unpredictable condition of grace depends?

RENIÉ: On that which is above us. I called it God, personally, and others call it as they wish. But art, work, sensitivity and even passion will not replace this sort of inspiration that all true virtuosos feel and communicate to listeners; at the same time, it's dangerous for one's own preparation if it overcomes the heart, but it's a marvelous sensation; one is like a medium between heaven and earth.

INTERVIEWER: We thank you, Henriette Renié, for allowing us to relive those joys and artistic emotions with you; and for allowing us to hear the echo of the magnificent creativity that you give to the harp, to "your" harp.

Third interview:

Introduction: After having spread the love for the harp worldwide

with her respected talent as a virtuoso, with her compositions, and

with her teaching, Henriette Renié now plays only for her friends

and for her chosen students. She still develops her teaching, the

shape of her works, as well as her transcriptions. She has agreed to

speak with us about her lifetime, full of experiences.

INTERVIEWER: Henriette Renié, not only have you enriched

the repertoire of the harp with your compositions, but I believe that

you have also published many transcriptions; is that correct?

RENIÉ: Many, indeed. Already in my first recital, in 1892, I

had three in my program. One of these, a piece by Rameau entitled

L'Egyptienne, is still performed.

INTERVIEWER: The little classics, written for the harpsichord,

must be charming on the harp.

RENIÉ: They are very good; in these pieces, one finds the grace

and the charm of that period.

INTERVIEWER: Does the purely classical music lend itself as

well to transcription?

RENIÉ: Less than the early music. It's more difficult. For these,

I can only adapt them to the harp; however, with the Romantic works, and even some modern works, I feel less guilty about modifying them.

INTERVIEWER: Could we hear an example of an early music transcription?

RENIÉ: Something typical . . . the beginning of the *La mélodieuse* by Daquin, for example; it's from the seventeenth or eighteenth century. [*She played some measures of* La mélodieuse.]

INTERVIEWER: Indeed, we find the quality of the grace in it which you mentioned. What is the genre of music which you sometimes had to adapt?

RENIÉ: Virtuosic works by Liszt such as *Rêve[s] d'amour* and *Le rossignol*, where I sought these sonorous effects by modifying the writing in two passages. In *Un sospiro*, I just modified the cadenzas. It is true that this transcription had been strongly recommended by the pianist Philippe (still very famous in the United States), who said, "but why don't you transcribe *Un sospiro*; it is made for the harp—there are only arpeggios."

INTERVIEWER: Would it be possible to hear at least the first measures of this transcription, owed to the advice of a pianist, which is quite rare!

RENIÉ: It's a work that I love! The first phrase alone is magnificent [*She played the phrase*].

INTERVIEWER: It's heavenly! After that, words can't express anything more! Do your students play many transcriptions?

RENIÉ: ... yes... on the condition that they already know how to play the harp well. To perform sonorous effects, legato tones, detached tones, etc., one must often go against the technical rules written in the method of the instrument.

INTERVIEWER: Yes, it's the exception that makes the rule.

RENIÉ: That's it, if you'd like. In summary, we are forced to. . . "disguise."

INTERVIEWER: Does the public like transcriptions?

RENIÉ: Yes; . . . I often have just as much success with transcriptions as with works written for the harp. Not only I, but all harpists play the *Arabesques* by Debussy, *Clair de lune*, and other transcribed works. . . .

INTERVIEWER: By you?

RENIÉ: By me.

INTERVIEWER: In a sense, you were the "pioneer" of the harp!

RENIÉ: Some say so.

INTERVIEWER: But, speaking of Debussy, the [*Danse sacrée et danse profane*]* were originally written for the harp, correct?

---

* This work was noted as *Danses sacrées et danses profanes* in the typescript of this interview.

RENIÉ: For the chromatic harp! But I adapted them, and I gave their first performance [on pedal harp] in 1910, under the direction of Camille Chevillard.

INTERVIEWER: What was your connection to the chromatic harp?

RENIÉ: My family had a friendly relationship with the inventor of the chromatic harp; in a way, I'm even a bit the cause of his invention.

INTERVIEWER: No?

RENIÉ: But yes. I was asked to play one evening for some friends, and M. Lyon was there. I was fourteen; it was the first year in which I played without the pedal extensions which complicated my performance a bit. I told him: "The difficulty of the harp is mainly the pedals, without which it would be a lot easier than the piano, but due to the pedals. . . ." Then he answered, "I'll try to invent a harp without pedals for you," and I replied: "If you do this, you'll do something!"

INTERVIEWER: This was an impulsive wish!

RENIÉ: Ah! And how!

INTERVIEWER: A few years later, you saw the development of this chromatic harp?

RENIÉ: Yes, and worse yet, I even competed against it, and very seriously and efficiently. For example, I performed at the Exhibit of Brussels in 1897, where Érard had sent me to demonstrate their harp.

I was there in the booth, playing every day, which bored me. But oh well. . . . I pretended that I looked like a trained monkey. . . . it didn't do anything! I played every day, and of course, when I was there, the chromatic harp would never dare be heard at the same time.

INTERVIEWER: Because the chromatic harp had its booth in front of yours?

RENIÉ: Across, exactly! You see, they weren't playing [the chromatic harp] when I started to play! Then, I played a trick on them: I conspicuously left the booth which represented Érard; then I silently came back from behind the booth. I had instructed one of my students, "When you see me come back, you'll wait until the chromatic harp has finished a piece heard and then you'll ask me to play."

INTERVIEWER: An elaborate plot!

RENIÉ: It's elaborate, isn't it? Then, I remember that he played the *Le noyer*, a small transcription by Schumann. As soon as it was over, my student asked me, "Couldn't you play something for us?" I went to my harp and I sounded with all that I had. Everyone turned around and of course, the poor chromatic harp was left alone on the spot!

INTERVIEWER: You are the pedal harp's champion since you have codified your experiences in a method?

RENIÉ: Yes, in 1940 the publisher Alphonse Leduc asked me to "codify" my method; he used the same term as you.

INTERVIEWER: This method: is it an important work?

RENIÉ: Yes, as much for teachers as for the musical examples that are included. Naturally, the first volume teaches one to play the harp. The second volume teaches one how to adjust harp technique to the modern requirements of this beautiful instrument.

INTERVIEWER: It's very interesting, this design in two volumes which seem to oppose one another and which complete each other. If you had written this method at the beginning of your career, would you have conceived it in the same way?

RENIÉ: Oh! Not at all! But the foundation would have been more or less the same, but I am always improving and changing. I took my examples from everywhere, from all existing methods and even sometimes from the imperfections of my students!

INTERVIEWER: This is wise! Did you teach professionally at a young age?

RENIÉ: Yes, I first gave rehearsals to Hasselmans's harp class at the age of eleven. At twelve-and-a-half, I had my first student, a charming young woman who told me, "I have heard a lot about you and I'd like to take lessons from you."

INTERVIEWER: How did you answer?

RENIÉ: I'm going to get my mom.

INTERVIEWER: This was charmingly innocent.

RENIÉ: This didn't prevent me from being a very strict professor right away, probably because I was afraid to be treated like a child.

INTERVIEWER: Yes, naturally. Was teaching important in your life?

RENIÉ: For me, teaching wasn't only a career, but it was also a type of mission as an art. Moreover, I owe it my greatest love.

INTERVIEWER: Did you stay in touch with your students who had become known artists themselves?

RENIÉ: I always have a great affection for them, even when they live far away, such as Marcel Grandjany, who remains a very dear friend.

INTERVIEWER: Do they often come back to visit you?

RENIÉ: A few years ago, a concert reunited three of my most brilliant students: Odette Le Dentu, Mildred Dilling and Solange Jean Renié, who have traveled around the world, spreading my method and sharing the love of the harp through their talent. There are so many more that I'd like to be able to name!

INTERVIEWER: Can harpists assist composers in writing for the harp?

RENIÉ: I did it many times. Composers came to me with their manuscripts, some of which even stayed with me. My old friend Philippe Gaubert, with whom I had so often worked with as a flutist, had long collaborated on his *Légende.* It is dedicated to me, and it was just performed at the competition of the Conservatoire.

INTERVIEWER: This year?

RENIÉ: This year. Thanks to the manuscript that I found, I certainly corrected a few printing errors after twenty-five or thirty years!

INTERVIEWER: That's interesting. Since you're talking about the competition, what do you think about it (if it's not too indiscreet)?

RENIÉ: There is a shining star: the *premier prix* revealed her "*hors concours*" (out of competition), with a unanimous vote.

INTERVIEWER: What's her name?

RENIÉ: A young American, Susann McDonald. She has exceptional artistic talent, warmth, and a contained sensitivity which has already conquered the Parisian public several times. She is one of the great virtuosos, I dare say.

INTERVIEWER: What class did this brilliant *lauréate* come from?

RENIÉ: She came from my friend Lily Laskine. We get along very well, both seeking to serve the ideal of the harp—and our students!

INTERVIEWER: It's very beautiful, this comraderie in art. On an artistic level do you think that the artist should consider the taste of the usual audience in the choice of his or her repertoire?

RENIÉ: Not at all in my opinion! We are to form and elevate the taste of the public, rather than bending toward it. Otherwise, it would be the end of art!

INTERVIEWER: Indeed, this seems applicable to all arts. In your opinion, is divine beauty the common quality that is shared by art forms?

RENIÉ: I am convinced of it: in all the arts, there is expression of the soul; even artists who do not believe receive this supernatural release without knowing it.

INTERVIEWER: Yes, the artist is a messenger, who sometimes ignores himself. By the way, Henriette Renié, when you think back on your beautiful and rich career, what feelings do you have?

RENIÉ: A feeling of amazed gratitude toward Providence, and remarkable memories, but it is as if they are detached from my present personality; when I speak of the past, it seems like it is about another person. That's how I can do it in all simplicity.

INTERVIEWER: However, you still bring the same zeal to your teaching!

RENIÉ: Yes, maybe even more! I not only work for myself, now. I work for those who are going to continue after me. For an artist, I believe that the hope of passing the torch onto other hands, far from saddening him or her, on the contrary gives peace and joy to his or her life!

[*Musical end with the third episode of* Pièce symphonique.]

This list of compositions and transcriptions has been compiled based on the currently available lists of Mlle Renié's works. The sources for this list are as follows:

Montesquiou, Odette de. *Henriette Renié et la harpe.* Paris: Josette Lyon, 1998.

Palkovic, Mark. *Harp Music Bibliography Supplement: Compositions for Solo Harp and Harp Ensemble.* Lanham, MD: Scarecrow Press, 2002.

Renié, Henriette. *Complete Method for Harp,* trans. Geraldine Ruegg. Paris: Leduc, [1966].

Varennes, Françoise des. *Henriette Renié, Living Harp,* 2d. ed. Translated by Susann McDonald. Bloomington, IN: MusicWorks-Harp Editions, 1990.

When possible, dates of composition (comp.), transcription (trans.), first performance (first perf.) and editing (ed.) have been provided after each title. The primary sources for the dates of composition are Renié's handwritten lists of works (Box 28, Folder 3). The sources for dates of first performance are the concert programs (various boxes) preserved at the International Harp Archives:

Henriette Renié (1875–1956) and Françoise des Varennes (1919–2004) Papers, International Harp Archives, Music Special Collections, Harold B. Lee Library, Brigham Young University, Provo, UT.

Some of the handwritten lists of Renié's works have dates beside them with no indication of what they refer to. In these cases, only the date has been noted in parentheses following the title in the list below. If multiple dates were found, even if they are contradictory, they have been listed together in parentheses. If no dates were available for a work, none have been listed.

The following lists contain works that are currently published, works that are now out of print, and works that may have existed only as manuscripts during Renié's lifetime. Next to those works that are currently unavailable, the note "not seen" appears in parentheses. If the source of a transcription was ambiguous, the note "not yet identified" appears in parentheses. In addition to these works, a list of Mlle Renié's transcriptions for harp ensemble may be found in Renié's biography by Françoise des Varennes, *Henriette Renié: Living Harp,* translated by Susann McDonald.

Method

Méthode complète de harpe, in 2 volumes (Paris: Leduc, 1946)
Complete Method for Harp, English translation by Geraldine Ruegg (Paris: Leduc, [1966])
Vol. 1: *Technique* (Technique)
Vol. 2: *Syntaxe-Appendice* (Syntax-Appendix)

Compositions

Andante religioso (comp. 1895)
(Religious Andante)
for harp and violin (or cello)

Ballade fantastique: d'après Le cœur révélateur d'Edgar Poe (first perf. 1907,
1910, ed. 1912)
(Fantastic Ballad: based on "The Tell-Tale Heart" by Edgar Allan Poe)
for harp

Concerto en ut mineur (first perf. 1901)
(Concerto in C Minor)
for harp and orchestra
also: reduction for harp and piano, and reduction of 1st movement for harp
with string quartet and double bass ad lib.

Contemplation (1898, 1900)
for harp

Danse des lutins (comp. 1911, first perf. 1912)
(Dance of the Goblins)
for harp

Deuxième ballade (first perf. 1911, 1912)
(Second Ballad)
for harp

Deux pièces symphoniques
(Two Symphonic Pieces)
for harp and orchestra, and reduction for harp and piano
1 *Elégie* (Elegy) (first perf. 1906)
2 *Danse caprice* (Capricious Dance) (first perf. 1907)

Fêtes enfantines
(Children's Celebrations)
for harp and narrator, ad lib.
(not seen)
1 *La vierge à la crèche* (The Virgin at the Crib)
2 *Mascarada* (Masquerade)
3 *Cloches de Pâques* (Bells of Easter)

Feuillets d'album
(Album Leaves)
for harp
  1 *Esquisse* (Sketch)
  2 *Danse d'autrefois* (Dance of the Past)
  3 *Angélus* (Angelus)

Feuilles d'automne *(Esquisse)* (first perf. 1912)
(Autumn Leaves [Sketch])
for harp

Grand-mère raconte une histoire: *petite pièce très facile pour la harpe*
  sans pédales (comp. 1926)
(Grandmother Tells a Story : a small easy piece for harp without pedals)

Légende: *d'après Les elfes de Leconte de Lisle* (comp. 1901, first perf. 1902)
(Legend: based on [the poem] "The Elves" by Leconte de Lisle)
for harp

Op. 1 (Six pièces)
(Six Pieces)
  1st Suite:
    1 *Menuet* (Minuet)
    2 *Au bord du ruisseau* (At the Edge of the Brook)
    3 *Petite valse* (Little Waltz)
  2nd Suite:
    4 *Air ancien* (Ancient Air)
    5 *Lied* (Song)
    6 *Valse mélancolique* (Melancholy Waltz)

Op. 2 (Six pièces brèves) (comp. 1919)
(Six Short Pieces)
  1st Suite:
    1 *Conte de Noël* (Tale of Christmas)
    2 *Recueillement* (Meditation)
    3 *Air de danse* (Dance Tune)
  2nd Suite:
    4 *Invention dans le style ancien* (Invention in the Ancient Style)
    5 *Rêverie* (Daydream)
    6 *Gavotte*

Pièce symphonique: en trois episodes (1907, first perf. 1909)
    (Symphonic Piece: in three episodes)
    for harp

Les pins de Charlannes: petite pièce très facile pour la harpe, sans
    pédales, avec piano ou seconde harpe (comp. 1928)
    (The Pines of Charlannes: a small easy piece for harp without pedals, with
    piano or second harp)

Près d'un berceau (comp. 1897)
    (Near a Cradle)
    for harp and narrator
    (not seen)

Promenade matinale: 2 pièces pour harpe (comp. 1913)
    (Morning Walks : two pieces for harp)
        1 *Au loin, dans la verdure, la mer calme et mystérieuse. . . .*
            (In the distance, in the greenery, the calm and mysterious sea. . . .)
        2 *Dans la campagne ensoleillée, la rosée scintilla. . . .*
            (In the sunny countryside, the dew glistened. . . .)

Scherzo-Fantaisie (comp. 1895)
    for harp (or piano) and violin

Sonate (1915)
    for piano and cello
    (not seen)

Trio (comp. 1901, first perf. 1905)
    for harp (or piano), violin, and cello

Transcriptions for solo harp
(not included in *Les classiques de la harpe*)

Albéniz, Isaac	*Le printemps* and *L'automne* (Spring and Autumn) from *Album of Miniatures* (also published as *Les saisons*, op. 201) Originally for piano

Bach, Johann Sebastian   *Pièce en sol (Præmbulum)* (trans. 1910)
Praeambulum, from *Partita no. 5*, BWV 829
Originally for harpsichord

Bosch, Jacques   *Passacaille: sérénade pour guitare*
Originally for guitar, with violin part by
Charles-François Gounod, ad lib.
(not seen)

Chabrier, Emmanuel   *Habanera*
Originally for piano (and arranged for
orchestra)

Couperin, François   *La commère*
From *Second livre de pièces de clavecin 6ᵉ
ordre*
Originally for harpsichord
(not seen)

Debussy, Claude   *Clair de lune* (trans. 1907)
From *Suite bergamasque*
Originally for piano
(not seen)

Danse sacrée et danse profane (trans. 1910,
first perf. 1910)
Transcribed for double-action pedal harp
Originally written for chromatic harp

Deux arabesques (trans. 1906, first perf. 1911)
Originally for piano

En bateau: extrait de la Petite Suite (trans. 1908)
from *Petite suite*
Originally for piano (4 hands)

La fille aux cheveux de lin
from *Préludes,* Bk. 1
Originally for piano
(not seen)

Dubois, Théodore	*Les abeilles* Originally for orchestra (not seen)
	Les myrtilles. . . from *Poèmes sylvestres*, Vol. 2 Originally for piano (not seen)
	Ronde des archers and *Stella Matutina* from *Deuxième suite : pour instruments à vent* Originally for 2 flutes, oboe, 2 clarinets, horn, and 2 bassoons (not seen)
	Sorrente from *20 pièces nouvelles de piano* Originally for piano
	Trois Morceau[x] (not seen, not yet identified)
Durand, Marie Auguste	*Première valse,* op. 83 from "Two Waltzes" Originally for piano (not seen)
Granados, Enrique	*Valses poéticos* Originally for piano (not seen)
Lyadov, Anatoly **Konstantinovich**	*Tabatière à musique* Originally for piano (not seen)
Liszt, Franz	*Un sospiro (Caprice poétique)* from *Trois [grandes] études de concert*, no. 3 (A. 118, S. 144, R. 5) Originally for piano

Mozart, Wolfgang Amadeus   *Sonate*
Originally for piano and violin
(not seen, not yet identified)

Sonate en ré
(not seen, not yet identified)

Périlhou, Albert   *Chanson de Guillot Martin*
from *Chants de France*
Originally for piano and voice, harmonized by
Périlhou
(not seen)

Prokofiev, Sergei   *Prélude*
Prelude no. 7, from *Ten Piano Pieces,* op. 12
Originally for piano (or harp)
(not seen)

Rameau, Jean-Philippe   *L'Egyptienne* (trans. 1897)
from *Nouvelles suites de pièces de clavecin,*
Suite no. 2
Originally for harpsichord

Respighi, Ottorino   *Siciliana*
from *Antiche danze ed arie per liuto* [P. 114]
Originally for piano; parts were later arranged
by the composer for string quartet, Suite no. 3
[P. 172a]
(not seen)

Scarlatti, Domenico   *Capriccio*
Sonata in E Major (K. 380, F. 326, L. 23)
Originally for harpsichord

Séverac, Déodat de   *En vacances = Holiday time = Ferien: petites
pièces romantiques de moyenne difficulté pour
piano*
from *1er Recueil* (1st collection)
Originally for piano
(not seen)

Renié's Transcriptions (*Les classiques de la harpe*)

The following list of transcriptions comes from that which was printed with Mlle Renié's twelve volumes of *Les classiques de la harpe*. The original title of each work is shown on the first line as it appeared in the original transcriptions (including printer errors in some cases), followed by the date of transcription when available. Where appropriate, corrected or alternate titles follow in square brackets along with the name of the collection from which the work comes. Catalog numbers have been included for ease of reference.

1ᵉʳ Recueil (Volume 1)
1ᵉʳ, 2ᵉ et 3ᵉ degrés (1ˢᵗ, 2ⁿᵈ, and 3ʳᵈ levels)

Rameau, Jean-Philippe	Musette (*Les Indes Galantes*) [Musette et rondeau from *Les Indes galantes, ballet, réduit à quatre grands concerts*, Premier concert]
	Menuet (*Castor et Pollux*) [from *Nouvelles suites de pièces de clavecin*, Suite no. 2]
	Menuets (*Platée*) [Menuets 1 and 2, from Act II, Scene 4]
Marais, Marin	Romance et Rondeau [not yet identified]
Daquin, Louis-Claude	La mélodieuse (trans. 1920) [from *Premier livre de pièces de clavecin*, Suite no. 4]
Beethoven, Ludwig van	Andante (*Sonate en sol majeur*) [from Piano Sonata no. 25, op. 79]
Haydn, Franz Joseph	Menuet (*33ᵉ Sonate*) (1900, 1908) [*Menuetto* from *Divertimento per il cembalo solo*, H. XVI: 6]

165

2ᵉ Recueil (Volume 2)
4ᵉ et 5ᵉ degrés (4th and 5th levels)

Daquin, Louis-Claude

L'Hirondelle (1904, 1905)
[from *Premier livre de pièces de clavecin,* Suite no. 2]

Zipoli, Domenico

Sarabande et Gigue
[*"Sarabanda e Giga"* from *Sonate d'intavolatura,* parte seconda *(Six Suites of Italian Lessons),* no. 2]

Scarlatti, Domenico

Pièce en ré (trans. 1910)
[Sonata in D Major, K. 430, F. 376, L. 463]

Lully, Jean-Baptiste

Célèbre Gavotte en Rondeau (*Ballets du roy*)
[not yet identified]*

Mendelssohn, Felix

Barcarolle (*Romance sans paroles n° 6)*
[*"Venetianisches Gondellied (Barcarolle)"* from *Lieder ohne Wörte I,* op. 19b, no. 6]

Chopin, Frédéric

Préludes nᵒˢ 20 et 23 (trans. 1910)
[from *24 Préludes,* op. 28]

3ᵉ Recueil (Volume 3)
5ᵉ et 6ᵉ degrés (5th and 6th levels)

Rameau, Jean-Philippe

Tambourin (*Les fêtes d'Hébé*)
[from *Pièces de clavessin avec une méthode pour la mécanique des doigts,* Suite no. 1]

Rondeau des songes (trans. 1923)
[*"Sommeil: suit[e] de trio des songes en rondeau,"* from *Dardanus,* Act IV, Scene 2]

Daquin, Louis-Claude

Le coucou (trans. 1899)
[from *Premier livre de pièces de clavecin,* Suite no. 3]

Beethoven, Ludwig van

Adagio (*Sonate au Clair de lune*) (trans. 1897)
[from Piano Sonata no. 14, op. 27, no. 2, "Moonlight"]

---

* This work was not listed in: Bruce Gustafson, A thematic locator for the works of Jean-Baptiste Lully*: coordinated with Herbert Schneider's Chronologisch-thematisches Verzeichnis sämtlicher Werke von Jean-Baptiste Lully (LWV),* (New York: Performer's Editions, 1989). One should note that "Ballets du roy" is not a specific ballet title, and could refer to any of Lully's royal ballets.

Bach, J. S.	Bourrée (*Suite en ut pour violoncelle*) (trans. 1901) [*Bourrée I–II* from *Suite 3* of *Sechs Suiten* (for cello), BWV 1009]
Schubert, Franz	Moment musical n° 3 [from *Moments musicaux,* op. 94 (D. 780), no. 3]

4ᵉ Recueil (Volume 4)
6ᵉ degré (6th level)

Paradisi, Domenico	Toccata (*4ᵉ sonate pour clavecin*) (trans. 1913) [from *12 Sonatedi gravicembalo,* Sonata no. 6] Note: this piece was originally labeled "Sonata No. 4" in Mlle Renié's published transcriptions.
Mozart, W. A.	Sonate facile en ut [*Eine kleine Klavier Sonate für Anfänger,* K. 545]

5ᵉ Recueil (Volume 5)
5ᵉ, 6ᵉ et 7ᵉ degrés (5th, 6th, and 7th levels)

Handel, G. F.	L'Harmonieux forgeron [from *8 suites de Pièces pour le Clavecin (1. Sammlung), Air con Variazioni* from Suite no. 5, HWV 430, "The Harmonious Blacksmith"]
Dandrieu, Jean-François	Les fifres (*1ᵉʳ livre des pièces*) [Suite no. 4]
	Les tourbillons (*1ᵉʳ livre des pièces*) (trans. 1920) [Suite no. 2]
Liszt, Franz	Consolations n° 3 [LW. A111b (S. 172, R. 12)]

6ᵉ Recueil (Volume 6)
7ᵉ et 8ᵉ degrés (7th and 8th levels)

Couperin, François	Tic-toc-choc ou les maillotins (trans. 1917) [from *Troisième livre de pièces de clavecin, 18ᵉ ordre*]

Handel, G. F.	Gavotte variée (*2ᵉ Recueil, 8ᵉ Suite*) (trans. 1897) [from *9 suites de pièces pour le clavecin (2. Sammlung)*, *Gavotta* from Suite no. 8, HWV 441]
Beethoven, Ludwig van	Adagio *(Sonate pathétique)* (trans. 1904) [from Piano Sonata no. 8, op. 13]
Chopin, Frédéric	Prélude n° 2 [Prelude no. 3 from *24 Préludes,* op. 28] Note: this piece was labeled "Prelude no. 2" in Mlle Renié's published transcriptions.

7ᵉ Recueil (Volume 7)
7ᵉ, 8ᵉ, et 9ᵉ degrés (7th, 8th and 9th levels)

Rameau, Jean-Philippe	Gavotte (*Boréales*) [from *Boréades,* Act IV, Scene 4] Note: this piece was labeled as an excerpt of Rameau's "Boréalesin Mlle Renié's published transcriptions.
Scarlatti, Domenico	Presto *(20ᵉ Sonate en sol majeur)* [Sonata in G Major, K. 13, L. 486]
Schumann, Robert	L'Oiseau prophète ["Vogel als Prophet," from *Waldscenen*, op. 82, no. 7]
Chopin, Frédéric	Célèbre Valse dite du chat [from *3 valses pour le piano*, op. 64, no. 1, CT. 212, "Minute"]

8ᵉ Recueil (Volume 8)
7ᵉ, 8ᵉ, et 9ᵉ degrés (7th, 8th and 9th levels)

Liszt, Franz	Consolations n° 2 [LW. A111b (S. 172, R. 12)]
Dagincourt, François	L'Etourdie (*Rondeau*) [from *Pièces de clavecin, troisième ordre* (D Major), no. 29]
Scarlatti, Domenico	Allegrissimo (*4ᵉ Sonate*) [K. 113, F. 72, L. 345]
Mendelssohn, Felix	Fileuse (*Romance sans paroles n° 34*) [from *Lieder ohne Wörte* VI, op. 67, no. 4]

9ᵉ Recueil (Volume 9)
7ᵉ, 8ᵉ, et 9ᵉ degrés (7th, 8th and 9th levels)

Scarlatti, Domenico Capriccio (*Sonate en mi majeur*) (1907, 1916)
[Sonata in E Major, K. 20, L. 375]

Liszt, Franz Consolations n° 5
[LW. A111b (S. 172, R. 12)]

Chopin, Frédéric Préludes nᵒˢ 6 et 11 (trans. 1910)
[from *24 Préludes,* op. 28]

Liszt, Franz Le rossignol, *d'après la Mélodie russe d'Alabieff*
(based on a Russian melody by Alabieff)
[from *Deux mélodies russes* (*Arabesques,* no. 1,
A. 86, S. 250, R. 102/1,
C. 322]

10ᵉ Recueil (Volume 10)
8ᵉ et 9ᵉ degrés (8th and 9th levels)

Duphy, Jacques La Victoire (trans. 1892)
[from *Second livre de pièces de clavecin,* no. 1]

Scarlatti, Domenico Pastorale
[K. 9, L. 413]

Schumann, Robert Au soir (trans. 1906)
["*Des Abends,*" from *Fantasiestücke,* bk. 1, op.
12, no. 1]

Liszt, Franz Nocturne (*N° 3 des Rêves d'amour*)
[from *Liebesträume, 3 notturnos,* no. 3 (O lieb, o
lieb, so lang du lieben kannst), LW. A103, S. 541,
R. 211, C. 585]

11ᵉ Recueil (Volume 11)
5ᵉ et 6ᵉ degrés (5th and 6th levels)

Bach, J. S. Dix pièces:

1. [*Praeambulum* from *Neun kleine Präludien aus
dem Klavierbüchlein für Wilhelm Friedemann
Bach,* BWV 927]

2. [*Inventio 1* from *Inventionen (2stg.) und Sinfonien (3stg.)* (Invention no. 1), BWV 772]

3. [from *Sechs kleine Präludien* (Prelude no. 5), BWV 937]

4. [from *Sechs kleine Präludien* (Prelude no. 1), BWV 933]

5. [*Praeludium*, from *Neun kleine Präludien aus dem Klavierbüchlein für Wilhelm Friedemann Bach*, BWV 928]

6. [*Präludium in e* from *Fünf Präludium und Fughetten* (Prelude no. 3), BWV 900]

7. *Corrente*
[from *Partita 5* of *Sechs Partiten* (Partita no. 5), BWV 829]

8. [from *Sechs kleine Präludien* (Prelude no. 3), BWV 935]

9. *Passepied*
[*Passepied I en Rondeau and Passepied II* from *Englische Suiten* (Suite no. 5), BWV 810]

10. *Bourrée*
[from *Französische Suiten* (Suite no. 6), BWV 817]

12ᵉ Recueil (Volume 12)
5ᵉ et 6ᵉ degrés (5th and 6th levels)

Bach, J. S.

Dix préludes (*Clavecin bien tempéré*)
(from *Das wohltemperierte Klavier I–II*, "The Well-Tempered Clavier, Vol. 1 and 2"):

1. [*Praeludium 1,* from Vol. 1, BWV 846]

2. [*Praeludium 5,* from Vol. 1, BWV 850]

3. [*Praeludium 6,* from Vol. 1, BWV 851]

4. [*Praeludium 8,* from Vol. 1, BWV 853]

5. [*Preludio 12*, from Vol. 2, BWV 881]

6. [*Praeludium 15,* from Vol. 1, BWV 860]

7. [*Praeludium 15,* from Vol. 2, BWV 884]

8. [*Praeludium 17,* from Vol. 1, BWV 862]

9. [*Praeludium 20,* from Vol. 1, BWV 865]

10. [*Praeludium 21,* from Vol. 1, BWV 866]

PRIMARY SOURCES

Henriette Renié (1875–1956) and Françoise des Varennes
(1919–2004) Papers, International Harp Archives, Music
Special Collections, Harold B. Lee Library, Brigham Young
University, Provo, UT.

Recordings of Renié Playing her Own
Compositions and Transcriptions
Preserved at Brigham Young University, arranged alphabetically by title.
Solo performance by Renié, unless otherwise stated.

Renié, Henriette. *Concerto en ut mineur "Andante"* (Renié),
Moment musical (Schubert, Renié), *Prélude* (Prokofiev, Renié).
Handwritten title: "Andante concerto, Moment musical."
Phonorecord.

Concerto en ut mineur pour harpe et orchestre, parts 1 & 2
"Allegro risoluto" (Renié). L'Orchestre Philharmonique
de Paris ; G. Cloez, conductor. n.p.: Odéon 171.076, n.d.
Phonorecord.

Concerto en ut mineur pour Harpe et Orchestre parts 3 & 4
"Adagio" (Renié). n.p.: Odéon 171.077. n.d. Phonorecord.

Concerto en ut mineur (Renié), *Contemplation* (Renié), *Tic-toc-
choc* (Couperin, Renié), *Andante religioso et Scherzo-Fantaisie*
(Renié), *Pastorale et Capriccio* (Scarlatti, Renié), and *1er
Promenade matinale* (Renié). n.p.: Le Kiosque d'Orphée, n.d.
Phonorecord.

Contemplation (Renié) and *La Source* (Zabel). [New York]:
Columbia E11089, n.d. Phonorecord.

Etude de concert (Godefroid) and *Danse des lutins* (Renié). [New York]: Columbia D 6247, n.d. Phonorecord.

Feuilles d'automne (Renié), *Menuet* (Rameau, Renié), and *Le coucou* (Daquin, Renié). Odéon 166.088, n.d. Phonorecord.

La Source (Zabel), and *Contemplation* (Renié). n.p.: Odéon 171.098, n.d. Phonorecord.

Légende (Renié). n.p.: Odéon 171.061, n.d. Phonorecord.

Légende (Renié), *Elégie* (Renié), *Danse caprice* (Renié), *Sonata facile en ut* (Mozart, Renié), *Un sospiro* (Liszt, Renié), *Le rossignol* (Liszt, Renié), and *Première arabesque* (Debussy, Renié). H.R. 001. Phonorecord.

Menuet (Haydn, Renié) and *Valse en re bémol* (*Valse du chat*) (Chopin, Renié). n.p.: Odéon 166.231, n.d. Phonorecord.

Moment musical n° 3 (Schubert, Renié), *Danse des lutins* (Renié), *Pièce symphonique* (Renié), *Deuxième promenade matinale* (Renié), *Contemplation* (Renié) played by Sextet, *Consolation n° 3* (Liszt, Renié), *Nocturne n° 3 des Rêves d'amour* (Liszt, Renié), *Pièce de concert* (Büsser), and *La vierge à la crèche, Mascarada, Cloche de Pâques*, harp and narrator. Phonorecord.

Moment musical (Schubert, Renié), *La commère* (Couperin, Renié) and *Prélude* (Prokofiev). n.p.: Odéon 166.232, n.d. Phonorecord.

Siciliana (Respighi) and *L'hirondelle* (Daquin, Renié). n.p.: Odéon 166.089, n.d. Phonorecord.

SECONDARY SOURCES

Andriamboavonjy, Landy. "Henriette Renié: harpiste, compositeur, pédagogue." Mémoire de Maître, Faculté de Lettres de Lyon II, 1990. Not seen.

Bochsa, Robert Nicolas Charles, and Charles Oberthür. *Universal Method for the Harp.* Boston: Carl Fischer, 1912.

Brown, Maurice J. E. *Chopin: An Index of his Works in Chronological Order.* London: Macmillan, 1960.

Cho, Min-Jung. "An Analysis of Renié's Works: *Symphonic Piece* and *Legend.*" D.A. document, New York University, 1995.

Deutsch, Otto Erich. *Schubert: Thematic Catalogue of All His Works in Chronological Order.* London: J. M. Dent & Sons Ltd., 1951.

Dilling, Mildred, and Virginia Morgan. "Henriette Renié." *The American Harp Journal* 5 (Summer 1975): 3–10.

_____. "Henriette Renié." *Harp News* 11 (Fall 1956): 5–6.

David Fuller, "Of Portraits, 'Sapho' and Couperin: Titles and Characters in French Instrumental Music of the High Baroque," *Music & Letters* 78 (May 1997): 167.

Govea, Wenonah Milton. *Nineteenth- and Twentieth-Century Harpists: A Bio-Critical Sourcebook.* Bio-Critical Sourcebooks on Musical Performance Series, ed. John Gillespie. Westport, CT.: Greenwood, 1995.

Gustafson, Bruce and Matthew Leshinskie. *A thematic locator for the works of Jean-Baptiste Lully: coordinated with Herbert Schneider's Chronologisch–thematisches Verzeichnis sämtlicher Werke von Jean-Baptiste Lully (LWV).* New York: Performer's Editions, 1989.

Han, June Y. "Harp Concerti Since 1925." D.M.A. document, The Juilliard School, 2004.

"Henriette Renié." *Harp News* 1, no. 3 (1951): 6, 13.

Higginbottom, Edward. "François Couperin," *The New Grove Dictionary of Music Online,* ed. Laura Macy; available from http://www.grovemusic.com; Internet. Accessed 27 May 2006.

Houser, Kimberly Ann. "Five Virtuoso Harpists as Composers: Their Contributions to the Technique and Literature of the Harp." D.M.A. document, University of Arizona, 2004.

Inglefield, Ruth K. *Marcel Grandjany: Concert Harpist, Composer, and Teacher.* n.p.: University Press of America, 1977. Reprint, Bloomington, IN: Vanderbilt Music Company, 1990 (page references are to the reprint edition).

Le Dentu, Odette. *A propos de . . . la harpe.* Paris: Billaudot, 1984.

Maxwell, Sally Calkins. "In Memoriam: Françoise des Varennes— September 21, 1919–March 18, 2004." *The American Harp Journal* 19 (Summer 2004): 57.

_____. E-mail interview by the author. 30 July 2006.

_____. "Reminiscences: Henriette Renié." *The American Harp Journal* 16 (Winter 1998): 53.

McDonald, Susann. Interviews by the author. 9 June 2006 (E-mail interview), and 28 July 2006 (personal interview).

Montesquiou, Odette de. "Henriette Renié, 1875–1956." *Journal suisse de la harpe* 7 (Winter 1995–96): 4–10.

_____. *Henriette Renié et la harpe*. Paris: Josette Lyon, 1998.

_____. *The Legend of Henriette Renié* (*Henriette Renié et la harpe*), ed. Jaymee Haefner, trans. Robert Kilpatrick. Bloomington, IN: AuthorHouse, 2006.

Morley, John George. *Harp Playing.* n.p.: Author, 1918. Reprint, Marina Del Ray, CA: Safari Publications, 1997.

Neuls-Bates, Carol. *Women in Music: An Anthology of Source Readings from theMiddle Ages to the Present.* New York: Harper Torchbooks, 1982.

Palkovic, Mark. *Harp Music Bibliography: Chamber Music and Concertos.* Lanham, MD.: Scarecrow Press, 2002.

_____. *Harp Music Bibliography Supplement: Compositions for Solo Harp and Harp Ensemble.* Lanham, MD.: Scarecrow Press, 2002.

Piana, Dominique. "Dolce quasi arpa: Franz Liszt and the Harp." *The American Harp Journal* 19 (Summer 2003): 7–23.

Renié, Henriette. 21 September 1925. Interview transcript. American Harp Society Repository, Library of Congress, Washington, D.C. Not seen.

Renié, Henriette. *Complete Method for Harp,* trans. Geraldine Ruegg. Paris: Leduc, [1966].

_____. *Méthode complète de harpe.* Paris: A. Leduc, 1946.

_____. "Recollections of a Harpist," trans. Renée Blyth. *The American Harp Journal* 1 (Fall 1968): 16–20.

Rensch, Roslyn. *Harps & Harpists.* Bloomington, IN: Indiana University Press, 1989.

Ripin, Edwin. "Pièce croisée," *The New Grove Dictionary of Music Online,* ed. Laura Macy; available from http://www.grovemusic.com; Internet. Accessed 6 July 2006.

Salzedo, Carlos, and Lucile Lawrence. *Method for the Harp.* New York: G. Schirmer, 1929.

Sharpes, Rita. "Mildred Dilling." *The American Harp Journal* 8 (Winter 1981): 4–9.

Slaughter, Caroline. "Henriette Renié: A Pioneer in the World of the Harp." M. M. thesis, Rice University, 1992.

Varennes, Françoise des. "Henriette Renié." *The American Harp Journal* 5 (Winter 1975): 8–18.

_____. *Henriette Renié, harpe vivante.* Paris: Barré-Dayez Editeurs, 1983. Not seen.

_____. "Henriette Renié: Harpe Vivante," excerpts trans. Sally Maxwell. *The American Harp Journal* 9 (Winter 1984): 2–11.

_____. *Henriette Renié: Living Harp*, 2d. ed., trans. Susann McDonald. Bloomington, IN: MusicWorks-Harp Editions, 1990.

Winter, Robert. "Schubert, Franz." *The New Grove Dictionary of Music Online,* ed. Laura Macy; available from http://www.grovemusic.com; Internet. Accessed 27 May 2006.

Yeung, Ann. "Edits to Henriette Renié's *Ballade fantastique d'après "Le cœur révélateur" d'Edgar Poe.*" *The American Harp Journal* 20 (Summer 2006), 21–23, 26–27.

Yeung, Ann. "Edits to Henriette Renié's *Contemplation.*" *The American Harp Journal* 19 (Winter 2004), 19–22.

Zingel, Hans Joachim. *Harp Music in the Nineteenth Century,* trans. Mark Palkovic. Bloomington, IN: Indiana University Press, 1992.

Sound Recordings

Renié, Henriette. *A Tribute to Henriette Renié, Live Tribute Concert.* Susann McDonald, harp (recorded June 25, 1975). United States: [S. McDonald] D–CD 1002, [1980s]. Compact Disc.

_____. *Henriette Renié.* Xavier de Maistre, harp. Arles, France: Harmonia Mundi France HMN 911692, 1999. Compact Disc.

_____. *Henriette Renié 1875–1956, Playing her Own Compositions and Transcriptions for Harp.* Henriette Renié, harp (recorded 1928–1930). United States: Eugene Chapter of the American Harp Society [2000s]. Compact Disc.

_____. *OEuvres d'Henriette Renié: Compositions & Transcriptions, enregistrements historiques 1927–1955.* Henriette Renié, harp (recorded 1927–1955). France: Association Internationale des Harpistes AIH 02, 2004. Compact Disc.

Scores Cited

All musical examples have been reproduced with permission from the publisher.

Beethoven, Ludwig van. "Andante" (from Piano sonata no. 25, op. 79). In *Les classiques de la harpe,* vol. 1. Transcribed for harp by Henriette Renié. AL.20113. Paris: Leduc, 1950.

Couperin, François. *Tic-toc-choc ou les maillotins.* In *Les classiques de la harpe,* vol. 6. Transcribed for harp by Henriette Renié. Paris: Leduc, 1954.

_____. *"Le tic-toc-choc, ou les maillotins: Pièce croisée."* In his *Œuvres complètes de François Couperin.* Volume 4: Musique de clavecin III, ed. Maurice Cauchie, 307–11. 8143. Paris: Editions de l'Oiseau-Lyre, 1932.

Daquin, Louis-Claude. *L'hirondelle* (from *Pieces de Clavecin*). In *Les classiques de la harpe,* vol. 2. Transcribed for harp by Henriette Renié. AL.20126. Paris: Leduc, 1950. Liszt, Franz. *Nocturne n° 3 des Rêves d'amour.* In *Les classiques de la harpe,* vol. 10. Transcribed for harp by Henriette Renié. AL.20167. Paris: Leduc, 1956.

_____. *"Notturno no. 3."* In his *Neue Ausgabe sämtlicher Werke.* Serie I: *Werke für Klavier zu zwei Händen,* ed. Dr. Zoltán Gárdonyi and István Szelényi, 60–64. Z.8253. Kassel: Bärenreiter, 1982.

Mozart, Wolfgang Amadeus. *Sonate facile en ut.* In *Les classiques de la harpe,* vol. 4. Transcribed for harp by Henriette Renié. AL.20132. Paris: Leduc, 1954.

Renié, Henriette. *Concerto en ut mineur: pour harpe et orchestre.* AL.20159, G.T.464. Paris: Leduc, n.d. Harp and piano score.

_____. *Légende: d'après "Les elfes" de Leconte de Lisle.* AL.20016, L.R.146. Paris: Leduc, [1957].

_____. *Promenade matinale: 2 pièces pour harpe.* L.R.436. Paris: Rouhier, 1923.

_____. *Scherzo-Fantaisie: pour harpe (ou piano) et violon.* L.R. 46. Paris: Rouhier, n.d. Harp and violin score.

Schubert, Franz. "*Moment musical* no. 3." In his *Complete Works.* Volume 5, Series 11: *Fantasy, Impromptus and Other Pieces for Pianoforte Solo* (1888), ed. Julius Epstein, 8 (94)–(95) 9. F.S. 111. [Leipzig]: Breitkopf & Härtel, 1884–1897. Reprint, American Musicological Society–Music Library Association Reprint Series. New York: Dover, 1965 (page references are to the reprint edition).

_____. *Moment musical* no. 3. In *Les classiques de la harpe,* vol. 3. Transcribed for harp by Henriette Renié. A.L.20175. Paris: Leduc, 1950.

ENDNOTES

1   Article by Noel-Gallon, entitled "Henriette Renié, 1875–1956," n.d., Box
    23, Folder 2, Henriette Renié (1875–1956) and Françoise des Varennes
    Papers, Music Special Collections, Harold B. Lee Library, Brigham Young
    University, Provo, UT.

2   Mildred Dilling and Virginia Morgan, "Henriette Renié," *The American
    Harp Journal 5* (Summer 1975): 5.

3   Wenonah Milton Govea, *Nineteenth- and Twentieth-Century Harpists: A
    Bio-Critical Sourcebook*, Bio-Critical Sourcebooks on Musical Performance
    Series, ed. John Gillespie (Westport, CT: Greenwood Press, 1995), 229.

4   Who's Who in Music questionnaire, [1949–50], Box 28, Folder 6, Renié and
    Varennes Papers.

5   Odette de Montesquiou, *The Legend of Henriette Renié (Henriette Renié et
    la harpe)*, ed. Jaymee Haefner, trans. Robert Kilpatrick (Bloomington, IN:
    AuthorHouse, 2006), 1.

6   Ibid. See also: Françoise des Varennes, "Henriette Renié: Harpe Vivante,"
    excerpts trans. Sally Maxwell, *The American Harp Journal 9* (Winter
    1984): 3.

7   Varennes, "Henriette Renié: Harpe Vivante," excerpts trans. Sally Maxwell,
    The American Harp Journal, 3.

8   Françoise des Varennes, Henriette Renié: T, 2d. ed., trans. Susann
    McDonald (Bloomington, IN: MusicWorks-Harp Editions, 1990), 27. See
    also: Varennes, "Henriette Renié: Harpe Vivante," trans. Maxwell, *The
    American Harp Journal 9* (Winter 1984): 3.

9   Dilling and Morgan, "Henriette Renié," *The American Harp Journal*, 3.

10 Montesquiou, *Legend of Renié*, 4.

[11] Govea, 231.

[12] Dilling and Morgan, "Henriette Renié," *The American Harp Journal*, 3.

[13] First Interview with Henriette Renié, aired August 1965 [recorded 1955?], Box 28, Folder 6, Renié and Varennes Papers.

[14] Varennes, *Living Harp*, 29.

[15] First Interview with Henriette Renié, aired August 1965 [recorded 1955?], Box 28, Folder 6, Renié and Varennes Papers.

[16] Govea, 231.

[17] Who's Who in Music questionnaire, [1949], Box 28, Folder 6, Renié and Varennes Papers.

[18] The other two great events were Wieniawsky's award at ten years and Henri Fissol's prize at the age of thirteen for harmony, according to the handwritten "Biography" (Box 23, Folder 5A).

[19] Varennes, *Living Harp*, 33–4.

[20] Who's Who in Music questionnaire, [1949], Box 28, Folder 6, Renié and Varennes Papers. See also Montesquiou, *Legend of Renié*, 8.

[21] First Interview with Henriette Renié, aired August 1965 [recorded 1955?], Box 28, Folder 6, Renié and Varennes Papers.

[22] Varennes, *Living Harp*, 40.

[23] Montesquiou, *Legend of Renié*, 8.

[24] Who's Who in Music questionnaire, [1949], Box 28, Folder 6, Renié and Varennes Papers.

[25] Varennes, *Living Harp*, 41.

[26] Govea, 234.

[27] "Henriette Renié, 1875–1956" (Article by Noel-Gallon), n.d., Box 23, Folder 2, Renié and Varennes Papers.

28 Mildred Dilling and Virginia Morgan, "Henriette Renié," *Harp News* 11 (Fall 1956): 5.

29 Montesquiou, *Legend of Renié*, 70.

30 Ibid., 30.

31 Varennes, *Living Harp*, 50–1, 80.

32 Ibid., 80.

33 Montesquiou, *Legend of Renié*, 12.

34 Ibid.

35 Dilling and Morgan, "Henriette Renié," *The American Harp Journal*, 5.

36 Montesquiou, *Legend of Renié*, 12.

37 Ibid., 45.

38 Dilling and Morgan, "Henriette Renié," *Harp News*, 6.

39 Varennes, "Henriette Renié: Harpe Vivante" (trans. Maxwell), *The American Harp Journal*, 5.

40 Caroline Slaughter, "Henriette Renié: A Pioneer in the World of the Harp" (MM thesis, Rice University, 1992), 4.

41 Montesquiou, *Legend of Renié*, 37.

42 Dilling and Morgan, "Henriette Renié," *The American Harp Journal*, 5.

43 Ibid., 4.

44 Two letters announcing Mlle Renié as recipient of *Légion d'Honneur*, 1954, Box 21, Folder 2, Renié and Varennes Papers.

45 Susann McDonald, E-mail interview by the author, 9 June 2006. Renié's *Légion d'Honneur* award was first requested for her in 1922.

46 Min-Jung Cho, "An Analysis of Henriette Renié's Works: *Symphonic Piece* and *Legend*," (D.A. document, New York University, 1995), 10.

47 Françoise des Varennes also compiled a series of Mlle Renié's radio
    interviews in a published biography of her life entitled *Henriette Renié: La
    harpe vivante.*

48 Montesquiou, *Legend of Renié*, 17.

49 Varennes, *Living Harp*, 52.

50 Ibid., 52.

51 Ibid., 53.

52 Roslyn Rensch, *Harps and Harpists* (Bloomington, IN: Indiana University
    Press, 1989), 214–5.

    Epigraph. Meditation from August 15, 1925, from Varennes, *Living
    Harp*, 75.

53 Montesquiou, *Legend of Renié*, 45.

54 L'art musical review (vol. 2, no. 60), 18 June 1937, Box 24, Folder 8, Renié
    and Varennes Papers.

55 Concert Review, 10 February [1914?], Box 24, Folder 8, Renié and Varennes
    Papers.

56 "Commentaries 1946" (Program notes), 12 May 1946, Box 28, Folder 6,
    Renié and Varennes Papers.

57 Concert Programs, Renié and Varennes Papers, passim.

58 Ibid.

59 Ibid., 61.

60 Program notes (typescript), n.d., Box 24, Folder 1, Renié and Varennes
    Papers.

61 Handwritten lists of works, n.d., Box 23, Folder 1, Renié and Varennes
    Papers.

62 "Playing Her Own Compositions and Transcriptions," n.d., Box 23, Folder 2,
    Renié and Varennes Papers.

63 Le guide du concert (vol. 8, no. 19), 10 February 1922, Box 24, Folder 1, Renié and Varennes Papers.

64 Ibid.

Epigraph. "Commentaries 1946" (Program notes), 12 May 1946, Box 28, Folder 6, Renié and Varennes Papers.

65 Montesquiou, Legend of Renié, 16.

66 Concert Programs, Renié and Varennes Papers, passim.

67 Second Interview with Henriette Renié, aired August 1965 [recorded 1955?], Box 28, Folder 6, Renié and Varennes Papers. See also Appendix C for portions of the interview transcript translated into English.

68 "Commentaries 1946" (Program notes), 12 May 1946, Box 28, Folder 6, Renié and Varennes Papers.

69 Ann Yeung, "Edits to Henriette Renié's *Contemplation,*" *The American Harp Journal* 19 (Winter 2004): 20.

70 Handwritten text for a speech by Renié, n.d., Box 9, Folder 12, Renié and Varennes Papers. See also: Yeung, "Edits to Henriette Renié's Contemplation," 19.

71 Dilling and Morgan, "Henriette Renié," *Harp News*, 5.

72 Sally Maxwell, E-mail interview by author, 7 July 2006.

73 Handwritten text for a speech by Renié, n.d., Box 9, Folder 12, Renié and Varennes Papers.

74 Susann McDonald, interview by the author, 28 July 2006.

75 Program notes (typescript), n.d., Box 24, Folder 1, Renié and Varennes Papers.

76 Susann McDonald, interview by the author, 28 July 2006.

77 Min-Jung Cho, "*Symphonic Piece* and *Legend,*" 7.

78 Susann McDonald, E-mail interview by the author, 9 June 2006.

[79] Program notes, 23 January 1932, Box 9, Folder 15, Renié and Varennes Papers.

[80] Program notes, n.d., Box 30, Folder 1A, Renié and Varennes Papers.

[81] Program notes, 23 January 1932, Box 9, Folder 15, Renié and Varennes Papers.

[82] First Interview with Henriette Renié, aired August 1965 [recorded 1955?], Box 28, Folder 6, Renié and Varennes Papers.

[83] Montesquiou, *Legend of Renié*, 14.

[84] Second Interview with Henriette Renié, aired August 1965 [recorded 1955?], Box 28, Folder 6, Renié and Varennes Papers.

[85] Ibid.

[86] "Commentaries 1946" (Program notes), 12 May 1946, Box 28, Folder 6, Renié and Varennes Papers.

Epigraph. Third Interview with Henriette Renié, aired August 1965 [recorded 1955?], Box 28, Folder 6, Renié and Varennes Papers.

[87] Varennes, *Living Harp*, 80.

[88] Letter from Renié to Mercier, [1912], Box 21, folder 2, Renié and Varennes Papers.

[89] Susann McDonald, E-mail interview by the author, 9 June 2006.

[90] "Vichy" article, August 1913, Box 24, Folder 8, Renié and Varennes Papers.

Epigraph. Henriette Renié, *Complete Method for Harp*, trans. Geraldine Ruegg (Paris: Leduc, [1966]), 2.

[91] John George Morley, *Harp Playing* (n.p.: Author, 1918; reprint, Marina Del Ray, CA: Safari Publications, 1997), passim.

[92] Letter from Salzedo to Renié, [1947?], Box 26, Folder 3, Renié and Varennes Papers.

93 Renié, *Complete Method*, trans. Ruegg, 4. See also: "Hommage à Henriette Renié" from *l'association internationale des harpistes et amis de la harpe*, Spring 1973, Box 24, Folder 5, Renié and des Varennes Papers.

94 Carlos Salzedo and Lucile Lawrence, *Complete Method for the Harp* (New York: G. Schirmer, 1929), 2.

95 Renié, *Complete Method*, trans. Ruegg, 28–29.

96 Ibid., 8.

97 Carlos Salzedo and Lucile Lawrence, *Complete Method for the Harp* (New York: G. Schirmer, 1929), 6.

98 Robert Nicholas Charles Bochsa and Charles Oberthür, *Universal Method for the Harp* (Boston: Carl Fischer, 1912), 21.

99 Renié, *Complete Method*, trans. Ruegg, 32.

100 Ibid., 157–160.

101 Renié, *Complete Method* trans. Ruegg, 135.

102 Ibid., 133–7.

103 Ibid., 146.

104 Ibid., 181.

105 Third Interview with Henriette Renié, aired August 1965 [recorded 1955?], Box 28, Folder 6, Renié and Varennes Papers.

106 Third Interview with Henriette Renié, aired August 1965 [recorded 1955?], Box 28, Folder 6, Renié and Varennes Papers.

107 Concert Programs, Renié and Varennes Papers, passim.

108 Ruth K. Inglefield, *Marcel Grandjany: Concert Harpist, Composer, and Teacher*, (n.p.: University Press, 1977; Bloomington, IN.: Vanderbilt Music Company, 1990), 34, 38.

[109] Typed program notes, n.d., Box 23, Folder 2, Renié and des Varennes Papers. *Note*: Together with Liszt's Nocturne no. 3 (*Rêves d'amour*), Mlle Renié referred to *Un sospiro* as her most challenging transcription for harp.

[110] Handwritten lists of works, n.d., Box 23, Folder 1, Renié and Varennes Papers.

[111] Maurice J. E. Brown, *Chopin: An Index of his Works in Chronological Order* (London: Macmillan, 1960), 159–61.

[112] Susann McDonald, interview by the author, 28 July 2006.

[113] Edward Higginbottom, "Françoise Couperin," *The New Grove Dictionary of Music Online*, ed. Laura Macy; available from http://www.grovemusic.com; Internet; accessed 27 May 2006.

[114] Edwin Ripin, "Pièce croisée," *The New Grove Dictionary of Music Online*, ed. Laura Macy; available from http://www.grovemusic.com; Internet; accessed 6 July 2006.

[115] François Couperin, *Œuvres complètes de François Couperin.,* Volume 4: *Musique de clavecin III*, ed. Maurice Cauchie, 307–11, 8143 (Paris: Editions de l'Oiseau-Lyre, 1932), 3.

[116] Handwritten lists of works, n.d., Box 23, Folder 1, Renié and Varennes Papers.

[117] François Couperin, *Œuvres complètes de François Couperin* , 3.

[118] Otto Erich Deutsch, *Schubert: Thematic Catalogue of All His Works in Chronological Order* (London: J. M. Dent & Sons Ltd., 1951), 360–361.

[119] Robert Winter, "Schubert, Franz," *The New Grove Dictionary of Music Online*, ed. Laura Macy; available from http://www.grovemusic.com; Internet; accessed 27 May 2006.

[120] Handwritten lists of works, n.d., Box 23, Folder 1, Renié and Varennes Papers.

[121] Ibid.

[122] Renié, *Complete Method*, trans. Ruegg, 4.

[123] Ibid., 14.

[124] Maxwell, E-mail interview by author, 7 July 2006.

[125] Varennes, *Living Harp*, 92.

[126] Yeung, "Edits to Henriette Renié's *Contemplation*," 22.

[127] Tribute by Marcel Grandjany, n.d., Box 23, Folder 5A, Renié and Varennes Papers.

INDEX

T

V

64, 65, 67, 68, 77, 116, 120, 123,

125, 126, 130, 137, 142, 145,

147, 148

About The Author

Jaymee Haefner's performances have been described by Daniel Buckley as possessing "an air of dreamy lyricism… interlocking melody lines with the deftness of a dancer's footwork." Jaymee joined the University of North Texas faculty in 2006 and serves as director of the UNT HarpBeats ensemble, Professor of Harp and Director of Undergraduate Studies for the College of Music. Her extensive performances include a feature at the 50th Anniversary of the American Harp Society (AHS) in New York City, and National Conference performances in New Orleans (2014), in Atlanta (2016) and performances throughout the Dallas–Fort Worth area, in Mexico, the Czech Republic and Russia. She has recorded with the Bloomington Pops Orchestra, baritone Daniel Narducci and Alfredo Rolando Ortiz. She published a biography (*The Legend of Henriette Renié)* and has performed and presented lectures for the World Harp Congress (WHC) in Prague, Sydney, Amsterdam and Hong Kong. Jaymee was Chairman of the 2011 AHS Institute and has served as the Secretary and Southwest Regional Director for the American Harp Society, Inc., has served as Treasurer and International Harp Associations Liaison for the WHC, and chair of the Harp Competition Task Force for the American String Teachers Association (ASTA). Dr. Haefner's projects include her "Better than One" duo with harpist Emily Mitchell and her "Crimson" duo with violinist Matt Milewski, including recent commissions for violin and harp. She obtained her Bachelor of Music and Master of Music degrees from the University of Arizona and her Doctor of Music degree from Indiana University Jacobs School of Music. When she isn't on stage, Dr. Haefner trains in karate with her son, and earned her first-degree black belt in 2015.